Problems in Philosophy

BELIEF AND KNOWLEDGE

Robert John Ackermann is professor of philosophy at the University of Massachusetts, Amherst, Massachusetts. He has been Fulbright Lecturer and Guggenheim Fellow in Philosophy. He has previously written *Theories of Knowledge* (McGraw-Hill, 1965), *Nondeductive Inference* (Routledge and Dover, 1966), *An Introduction to Many-Valued Logics* (Routledge and Dover, 1967), *Modern Deductive Logic* (Doubleday & Company, Inc. and Macmillan, 1970), *Philosophy of Science* (Pegasus, 1970), and he has contributed widely to professional journals.

Problems in Philosophy

BELIEF
AND KNOWLEDGE
by
ROBERT J. ACKERMANN

ANCHOR BOOKS

Doubleday & Company, Inc.

Garden City, New York

1972

Anchor Books edition: 1972

Library of Congress Catalog Card Number 79–175407
Copyright © 1972 by Robert John Ackermann
All Rights Reserved
Printed in the United States of America
First Edition

ACKNOWLEDGMENT

I would like to take this opportunity to thank Bruce Aune, Steven Braude, Fred Feldman, Edmund L. Gettier, and Michael Hooker for their willingness to discuss certain problems that arose in connection with setting my mind straight about knowledge and belief in the course of writing this monograph. There are some matters on which I still disagree with each of them, but without their help, I could not have written a manuscript with which I would have been satisfied, given the space limitations of this series.

I should like to dedicate this volume to the series general editor, D. J. O'Connor—left-handed spin bowler, Chelsea fan, philosopher, and friend.

CONTENTS

BELIEF AND KNOWLEDGE

Chapter 1

Kinds of Belief

A laboratory rat has been repeatedly introduced into a maze with two exits of differing shape, one rectangular and one circular. In previous trials, the relative positions of the two exits has varied, but food has appeared only behind the circular exit. Released into the maze once again, the rat proceeds to exit directly through the circular exit. Does the rat believe that food is to be found behind the circular exit? Philosophers have generally agreed that the answer to this question involves conceptual problems about the nature of belief. In other words, whether we want to say that the rat does or does not believe anything in this situation is at least partially determined by what we may wish to regard as a belief in a clarified language used to describe mental states.

Many philosophers have decided that it is best to deny that the rat has or entertains any beliefs. Although the rat is said to behave *as if* it had beliefs, this can be dismissed as an anthropomorphism that would be circumvented in an adequate rat neurophysiology by description of some mechanism causing the rat's behavior. On this view, what we call belief is to be conceptually related to linguistic competence of some kind. One line of defense for this position is to point out that human belief in various paradigm cases is associated with conscious formulation of a belief sentence, or at the very least with the ability to formulate such a sentence if certain questions are asked of the believer. It is argued that the behavior of the rat, by contrast, could be duplicated by an easily conceived mechanism. We construct a small mechanical rat capable of self-guided locomotion which employs a scanning device capable of distinguishing between a rectangular and a circular exit. The mechanical rat is also provided with a learning program that sharply increases exiting behavior through the circular exit if food is found behind it but not behind the rectangular exit. A mechanical rat of this complexity lies easily within current computer technology. After construction and prior trials, a release of the mechanical rat into the same maze used earlier in the rat experiment results in unerring disappearance through the circular exit. In fact, after dressing up the mechanism with a little fur and some tape-recorded rat noises, it could become nearly impossible to tell from a short distance whether the animal or its mechanical counterpart is actually running the maze. Let us grant this modest piece of science fiction completely. Most philosophers would then agree that the mechanical rat cannot believe anything, hence a fortiori cannot believe anything about the relationship between the shape of exits and food.

We can abstract a more compact argument from the description of the mechanical rat once we have granted the possibility of its construction. An a priori or conceptual premise is that belief must be associated with consciousness, or at least with the kind of consciousness associated with certain linguistic abilities. It follows from this premise and certain common-sense observations about the mechanical rat that the mechanical rat is not conscious at all, and so cannot believe anything. From the fact that the observed behavior of the two rats in the maze is indistinguishable, one can then argue persuasively that there is no reason to attribute consciousness to the animal, and hence that the animal is best conceived as a very sophisticated mechanism that operates entirely without beliefs. This argument cannot establish that the animal has no beliefs. Rather, it suggests that there is no reason to posit beliefs of the rat, so that the burden of proof lies with anyone who argues that beliefs *can* be attributed to rats for some coherent purpose and, in fact, should be attributed to them. Obviously, the suggestion of this small argument is that all non-human animal species that lack appropriate linguistic ability (and this may include all non-human species) are such that their behavior can be modeled by sophisticated mechanisms, and hence their behavior does not require the postulation of beliefs for purposes of scientific explanation.

Now let us consider another rat, in this case a low-grade human being whom we shall call Harvey Prol. Harvey regularly beats his wife and kids, is nasty to his fellow custodians at the munitions plant, never says anything that anyone finds interesting, drinks away most of his small income, refuses to make small repairs to his house, and so forth. Harvey is watching the Red Sox play the Yankees. During a commercial break, he rises from his chair, hits a couple of the kids, opens the refrigerator, and without looking inside, expertly grabs a can of beer from the top shelf. The top shelf is the only shelf to contain beer, and it contains the remains of two six packs that Harvey placed there to carry him through the ball game. Did Harvey believe when he rose that there was a beer for him on the top shelf of the refrigerator? Again, there can be a division of opinion. Most people would probably say that Harvey did believe that there was beer waiting for him. Harvey's behavior has been chosen for ease of simulation. We could conceive of a mechanical Harvey who would sense commercials, proceed to smack any members of his family within easy reach, and then grab a can of beer from the top shelf of the refrigerator. The simulation problem doesn't seem completely out of reach of the techniques already involved in producing the mechanical laboratory rat. Harvey can be distinguished from the mechanical rat on the grounds that Harvey has the capacity for linguistic expression of his beliefs and the rat does not. But for just the piece of behavior that has been described, this capacity doesn't seem to matter. A mechanical Harvey might behave just like Harvey, and we could know from our construction of the machine that the machine was not conscious. As in the case of the rat in the maze, this would give us reason to suspect that the capacity for linguistic expression is not essentially involved.

Some philosophers have held that everything is explainable in principle by the laws of physics (some of which may yet be discovered). Such philosophers may hold human beings to be merely sophisticated mechanisms. On such a view, linguistic competence is a reflection of sophistication in design, but not of a break with an animal past. There may be physiological mechanisms that show that animals and humans share a kind of belief structure which could be explained in an advanced science of animal behavior. This is, of course, opposed to the view mentioned earlier that linguistic capacity entails a sharp distinction between *all* human belief and any conception of animal belief. It is clear that parts of these views (somewhat altered) can be combined to give a variety of views about human and animal belief.

In this monograph, we will be interested primarily in human belief, and consequently we will not need to make any decisions about animal belief, whether or not it exists in some sense, and if so how it compares to human belief. But it does seem to be important to establish that there are human beliefs like that exhibited by Harvey, beliefs that are revealed in action but may not be accompanied by any conscious formulation of the belief. Indeed, based on the sketch of Harvey's activities, it will be flatly asserted that there are such beliefs. In this sense, we often describe the behavior of others *as if* they held certain beliefs even though our evidence for this may be no different in kind than that which is used in the case of belief ascriptions to animals. It is true that we probably perceive human beings somewhat differently, as possessing certain complex linguistic dispositions, for example, and we will have to assume that this can be ignored for certain circumscribed bits of behavior. We will call such beliefs *behavioral* beliefs to indicate that they can be discerned in the behavior of others.

Behavioral beliefs are not discerned simply because there are fixed behavior patterns that anyone holding a certain belief will exhibit. How a man will behave, given that he has certain beliefs, is partly determined by his personality and character and partly determined by the context. Harvey's reaching for a beer on the top shelf is sufficient evidence that he believes a beer to be there. Tom, who doesn't like beer and doesn't want one, won't reach for a beer even if he thinks that one awaits. Bob, who likes beer and desperately wants one, reaches for the orange juice on the second shelf because the vicar has dropped in for a chat about the building fund. All of these actions may be as nearly reflexive as a postulated psychological theory will allow. In any event, we can easily suppose that none of these agents has thought out a line of action on a conscious level. Given these complexities, can we ever be sure that we have correctly identified a behavioral belief? If we know the agent well and understand the circumstances, we can often read the agent's beliefs in what he does. This is not intended to be trivial since it suggests that behavioral belief may be read only by someone who knows the personality and character of the agent, and can there-fore make a good guess as to the agent's perception of the circumstances in which he finds himself. We also have the supporting test of interrogation. If the agent is friendly and is not threatened by possible punishment, we can ask him about his beliefs and take the answers more or less at face value. This doesn't refute skepticism about knowing the mental states of others, but refuta-tions of skepticism are available in quantity, and the reader is urged to take his choice. Here we will assume that human beings have beliefs and that we can often tell what they are. Our study will be primarily directed at determining whether all of the beliefs that we can at-tribute to some agent (at some time) are mutually com-patible.

The *behavioral beliefs* that have been described so far are not equivalent to what we often call *unconscious beliefs*. It is true that the agent acting on a behavioral belief does not consciously formulate it, but a behavioral belief has been taken as formulable by the human agent on reflection, or as recognizable by the agent in response to a query. The familiar unconscious beliefs are more typically beliefs that have been discussed in connection with psychoanalytic theory, and these beliefs do not yield their identities easily to reflection or to query. For our purposes, we will think of unconscious beliefs as rather long-standing beliefs that can influence behavior over a long period of time, but which resist recognition by the agent. Behavioral beliefs, by contrast, will be thought of as non-conscious rather than unconscious.

Behavioral beliefs will be assumed to be easily recognizable at the conscious level. The notion of behavioral belief is particularly important in human action where the agent encounters no difficulty, so that his beliefs do not require scrutiny or examination at the conscious level. Behavioral beliefs are *not* habits in the sense of the pragmatist. Habits, having typically once been conscious, are currently unconscious beliefs or perhaps even require a separate category. Note that Harvey need not have a habit of reaching for beer even though he does it frequently.

A man may have a belief (or beliefs) about some group of people amounting to a prejudicial attitude against them, yet believe that he has no such prejudicial attitude. Under these circumstances, we cannot expect the prejudice to appear in response to any simple question about its existence. The agent may have an explanation (rationalization) of every specific act of his involving prejudice which alludes only to possible motivations which do not involve prejudice. A man who excludes another man from some club on grounds of prejudice might consciously explain his action by saying that the man's qualifications for membership were not very good. We can, in this sense, delude ourselves, and this fact seems plain even if one cares to reject broad areas of psychoanalytic theory and explanation as a rather poorly grounded science.

Prejudice coupled with overt denial of prejudice may yield to therapeutic techniques. A man may come to see that various acts of his exhibit prejudice, and hence learn that he has a certain belief conflicting with a belief that he had previously taken to be his. Other unconscious beliefs may not yield to therapeutic techniques at all. Sufficiently deep beliefs about a person's own nature may not be capable of exposure while the agent retains the same character and personality. In this sense, unconscious beliefs are probably involved in our actions and mental states, all of which could not be listed in a philosophical inventory of our persons. Unlike behavioral beliefs, such unconscious beliefs cannot be read off from behavior except as the extended application of some psychoanalytic theory may permit.

We now introduce two further notions of belief which have proved very important in philosophical literature. First, we will call any belief a person has explicitly formulated, and which he is therefore aware of, a *conscious belief*. Conscious beliefs have been the kind most often discussed descriptively by philosophers. The first three kinds of belief that we have distinguished—behavioral, unconscious, and conscious—are all notions of belief that should be familiar to us on common-sense observation in a scientifically enlightened era. All men will typically have some beliefs of all three kinds which would be involved in any full explanation and description of their behavior.

The fourth kind of belief to be introduced, *rational belief,* is a philosophical idealization of actual belief structures as they are found in human beings, and this requires some discussion that goes beyond a common-sense picture of the beliefs that human beings hold. When philosophers discuss logic and develop logical systems, they are interested in an ideal kind of validity that is *not* exhibited in most of the arguments occurring in real life. The ideal serves as a standard that can be used in the critical assessment of actual belief structures. Rational belief will be an ideal standard for critical assessment, which no human being could actually exhibit.

The first and most obvious requirement of rational belief is that a set of particular beliefs which is to be regarded as rational be consistent. (What this means in detail will be developed in the next two chapters.) In addition, most philosophers have supposed that a rational set of beliefs should be complete in the sense that all of the logical consequences of a given consistent set of beliefs should be regarded as belonging to a rational set of beliefs. This completeness condition is strong since it plainly requires that a man having any belief also have as beliefs the infinite number of consequent beliefs that can be drawn from that belief by valid inference. The *completeness condition* reveals the essentially ideal nature of rational belief. Nonetheless, the introduction of consistency and completeness in this sense has a rather obvious motivation. If consistency is important, we might like to view a rational man as ideally consistent. This would mean, among other things, that he would not hold a pair of beliefs from which a contradiction could be derived, no matter how difficult or lengthy a task it might be to demonstrate that contradiction. If we include all of the logical consequences of the basic beliefs (in some sense) of a rational man in his rational belief set, we can find any contradiction in his beliefs by means of well-known and rather simple tests for logical consistency. Otherwise, a man might thwart our intuitions about rationality by simply refusing to draw the inferences required to establish inconsistency. The usual philosophical account of *rationality* has it that the rational man will accept any consequences of his beliefs licensed by valid logical inference. Once we have indicated how rational belief is to be conceived as an idealization, we may be interested in the connection between actual belief and this ideal counterpart. The approach should be nearly obvious. We will take a person's actual beliefs to be rational if they could be taken as a proper subset of the set of be-

liefs of some ideally rational agent whose rational belief structure satisfied the conditions of consistency and
completeness as well as other conditions that analysis
might suggest. An even weaker sense of rationality is
provided if we say a man is rational should he always
be willing to revise his beliefs when it is demonstrated
that they are not incorporable in the belief structure
of an ideally rational agent. The notion of *unconscious
belief* clouds any possibility of a total theory of belief
since it seems to preclude any enumeration of a person's actual beliefs. It would be quite enough for
philosophical purposes if we could show that a person's
conscious beliefs could be incorporated into an idealized
rational belief structure. Philosophers have worked
mostly on programs of this kind, attempting to develop
criteria for rational belief structures that will make the
notion of rational belief philosophically fruitful. In the
next two chapters, we will examine some of the more
important considerations regarding *rational belief structures* that philosophical analysis has uncovered.

Chapter 2

Consistent Belief

The complexity of actual human belief revealed by the kinds of belief we noted in the last chapter proves a nearly insuperable obstacle to philosophical analysis. There is literally no statement about human beliefs that holds true for the four kinds of belief we have noted, or even for any arbitrarily selected pair of kinds of belief. For example, consider the following claim:

> If person *a* believes that he believes that *p*, then he believes that *p*.

It is not clear that the antecedent makes sense for *behavioral belief* (believing that one believes seems to require the use of linguistic competence), and the claim is clearly false in general because of unconscious belief. A person may (consciously) believe that he believes that *p*, yet (unconsciously) believe that not *p*. In the face of these complexities, the strategy is to divide and conquer. The first restriction usually adopted in studying the consistency of belief is to consider only conscious belief and rational belief. This restriction brings immediate rewards. For example, the claim we have just been discussing is probably true for *conscious belief* and it is surely true (by hypothesis) for *rational belief*. We will explicitly adopt the restriction to conscious and rational belief in the next two chapters. A student who turns to the literature must be warned that a similar restriction is not always noted by authors, even when they have it in mind, so that the sense of belief that they are discussing and the possible truth of their claims must rest with a careful contextual reading. For practice, the reader might examine the following quotation out of context:

> If person *a* does not believe that *p,* he does not believe that he knows that *p.*

Is this true under all readings? Is it true under any reading?

The next phase of division prior to conquest is to restrict the beliefs being analyzed to a class of beliefs we will call factual beliefs. A *factual belief* is such that one can convince oneself of the truth or falsity of it by scientific or everyday observation. In real life, of course, human beings have aesthetic, ethical, and political beliefs (as well as many other kinds) that are not factual on the intended account. Grammatically, all of the following are in order:

(i)   I believe that the sun is shining.
(ii) I believe that the Bellows is the most beautiful painting in the collection.
(iii) I believe that I ought to pay for this even though they didn't charge me.

Under any natural reading, only (i) expresses a factual belief. Philosophers have been particularly careless in not noting that they were discussing conscious factual belief and rational factual belief. For the most part, they have been interested in an epistemology for science, or they have accepted some form of the fact-value dichotomy, and hence they have fallen naturally into a discussion solely of factual belief without noticing explicitly that their remarks could not apply to the full range of human belief. Again, we will explicitly adopt the restriction that beliefs to be discussed are factual beliefs. Later in the monograph, a few remarks will be made about the consequences of relaxing this restriction.

There is one kind of belief assertion that has not been discussed so far and will largely be ignored. Consider the following dialogue:

> *A:* Where are my skates?
> *B:* I don't know; I believe I last saw them in the hall closet.

Here *B* is not expressing a belief of any importance. *B*'s belief is admittedly only a guess or hunch under the circumstances, and *B* might well have said "I'd guess they're in the hall closet," or "I think they're in the hall closet." We will rule out, as a third restriction, any *conscious belief* of this kind that is but a guess under uncertain circumstances. We will concentrate on conscious beliefs that the agent definitely thinks are true.

A traditional way of approaching belief sentences has been to attempt an analysis of their logical form with an eye toward assessing the validity of inferences about beliefs. The apparent grammatical form of a belief sentence is similar to that of many other sentences. For example, the following pair of sentences may seem to have superficial grammatical similarities:

> (1) John believes that Tom is the best golfer in town.
> (2) John is standing to the left of Tom, who is the best golfer in town.

There are, however, well-known difficulties with attempting to work out a grammatical parallel. (2) is quite clearly about John and about Tom, and if (2) is asserted, it would say that a certain spatial relationship holds between John and Tom. The difficulty with (1) is that it is clearly about John, but it may not be about Tom at all, and hence it cannot (in general) express a relationship between John and Tom. The reason for this is that a person's beliefs can be, to put it in Bruce Aune's heterodox but suggestive phrase, crazy as hell. In this case, John may have a belief based on hearsay which was confused by John to the point where he believes that there is a person called Tom who is the best golfer in town when in fact there is no such person. If (1) were uttered by Dick to Harry, and Dick and Harry both know a person who is called Tom and who is a golfer, or at least a resident of the town, Dick may intend (1) to be about John and about Tom. But if John, Dick, and Harry are just driving through John's home town (which John but not Dick or Harry visits occasionally), (1) may be used by Dick to tell Harry that John has just said "Tom is the best golfer in town." In this case, Dick is probably not making the presupposition that Tom exists. To cover the general case, therefore, we cannot hold that a sentence like (1) is about John and about Tom, and says, if asserted, that some (complex) relationship exists between them.

In point of fact, the locution "x believes that—," when considered as a fragment of English, can be turned into a sentence by replacing x with the name of someone and inserting a declarative sentence into the blank. The truth or falsity of the sentence (or the related statement or proposition it is taken to express) that results is independent of the truth or falsity of the sentence inserted in the blank. Someone may believe something whether it is true or false, and it may be that someone does not believe something no matter how obviously true it is or how much evidence he has for its truth. This is what is meant by saying that beliefs can be crazy as hell. The more well informed and rational a person is, the more likely his beliefs are to be true, but we cannot infer that his beliefs are true because he holds them.[1] Again, because a person holds some belief we cannot infer that he holds any other belief without considerable additional information.

Since it seems that inferences about beliefs are rarely valid, one popular strategy for expressing the logical form of belief sentences compatibly with capturing the facts about inference is to treat belief sentences as ascribing a very complicated predicate to some person. We can express this informally by hyphenating a belief sentence in an appropriate fashion. Taking (1) as our example, we obtain the following by hyphenation:

(3) John believes-that-Tom-is-the-best-golfer-in-town.

The point of hyphenating is to show that *Tom* does not occur in a referential position; that is, that the sentence is about John (for whom a name occurs normally) but not about Tom. A name for Tom occurs only as an inseparable constituent of a complicated predicate which the sentence is analyzed as ascribing to John. (3) has the following logical form after abstraction:

(4) *Pa.*

In this formula *a* abstracts a name for John and *P* stands for the hyphenated predicate. The hyphenation policy captures the basic facts about belief inference. It is *conservative* in the sense that if we employ this strategy, we can never use our logic (construed here as some form of Standard Logic) to license inference from a true belief sentence to a false belief sentence. Indeed, it

[1] This has sometimes been supposed otherwise for non-human agents. For example, some theologians have held that God cannot have false beliefs.

won't license any but the most trivial inferences. So to speak, *Qa* can never follow from *Pa* since we can compatibly assign *Pa,* the value truth, on some interpretation and *Qa,* the value falsity, on the same interpretation with the usual semantics of Standard Logic.

The result that no inferences of this kind are valid may seem too strong. Although it might be true that there are no inferences that philosophers *generally* accept as valid for belief sentences, most philosophers accept the view that some inferences which they have singled out are valid. For example, a philosopher might feel that the following inference should be regarded as valid:

(5)   John believes that Tom is tall and thin.
        Therefore,
(6)   John believes that Tom is tall.

We need to really stretch our imaginations to feel that John might believe Tom tall and thin and yet not believe Tom tall, perhaps because John has not yet separated tall from thin in his mind. We might suppose that John is just learning English and hasn't yet mastered the grammar of *and.* (By contrast, if something is black and white, it isn't black.) A philosopher attracted to the hyphenated policy for expressing logical form might feel that on anybody's accounting of inferences that are to be kept, the inferences lost by the hyphenated policy are too few to worry about given the simplicity of the overall theory. He may also feel that if special care is taken in formalizing the tricky cases, the wanted inferences could be retained anyway. For example, someone who wanted to keep the inference from (5) to (6) could find (5) equivalent to the following:

(7)   John believes that Tom is tall and John believes that Tom is thin.

In this case, (6) would follow by simplification in Standard Logic. From the standpoint of this inference, therefore, the hyphenated policy could be kept and any inferences that seem wanted could be handled on a special basis.

Unfortunately for considering inferences in terms of special cases, *inferences* about beliefs are not the only concern of the philosopher. The logical form produced by the hyphenated policy is not very helpful from at least two viewpoints. First, there is the problem that we can compare beliefs in terms of their content, something that we must do in speaking and particularly in learning a language. Second, if someone asks John what he believes about Tom, John may provide a list as follows:

(8)   I believe that Tom is the best golfer in town.
(9)   I believe that Tom is tall.
(10) I believe that Tom is thin.
(11) I believe that Tom lives on Sunset Avenue.

.
.
.

These are all different beliefs, and none of them follows from any of the others. They are, however, all beliefs about Tom. The hyphenated policy obscures this. Hyphenated formalization of (8)–(11) obviously results in a series of formulae like the following:

(12) Ra
(13) Sa
(14) Ta
(15) Ua

.
.
.

This formalization, conservative as it is with respect to inference, completely loses the fact that there is something in common between the beliefs. It is not counter to tradition to look to logical form to exhibit common and diverse sentential structures, and so reveal something about relationships that are not merely inferential. We must recognize the sort of cross reference exhibited by the beliefs in (8)–(11) if we are to understand how these beliefs are related and what they can mean to John. The hyphenated policy is of very little help in this regard.

We have already seen that we cannot take (8)–(11) as about both John and Tom because Tom may not exist. (We will assume here that there is no question but that the Tom mentioned somehow in (8)–(11) is the same person if he does exist, so that there is no question about possible ambiguity.) The difficulty with un-hyphenating our analysis of belief sentences is that we must regard belief sentences as expressing complicated relationships between a person and some of his concepts, or between a person and various propositions, or something of this sort. Another possibility is to regard a belief sentence as expressing some sort of behavioral claim. None of these moves is entirely satisfactory. Take the last first. To say that John believes that Tom is the best golfer in town might conceivably just say something about John, namely, that he is disposed to say things like, "There goes the best golfer in town," whenever Tom (or somebody he thinks is the Tom he talks about) walks by. The difficulty here is that this strategy can provide no *general* account of what belief sentences may mean. A particular person might be disposed to act in calculable ways, but different people say different sorts of things in similar situations (suggesting that there is no accurate range of sentences on which the analysis can draw as likely to be uttered in the crucial circumstances), and some find it very difficult to speak at all in the same situations. Human variability seems to preclude the possibility of analysis of belief along any of the classical behaviorist lines.

The difficulty with the other type of analysis mentioned, that of taking beliefs as complicated relationships between people and individual concepts or propositions, is largely philosophical and ontological. Many philosophers have felt that individual concepts and propositions are very problematic entities whose existence is a matter of considerable dubiety. For these philosophers, talk about concepts or propositions would be translated in an adequate philosophical view about language into talk about some kind of entity (or entities) that would more clearly belong to the province of scientific investigation. Otherwise, postulation of the existence of these entities would seem to take us outside the realm of the physical world and to force us to adopt a dualism that is difficult to make intelligible in a world view whose major outlines are determined by modern science. The prima facie difficulty is that concepts and propositions are not clearly related to objects of scientific inquiry, having been postulated by philosophers to solve a range of philosophical puzzles about meaning. The sort of problem that gives rise to this attitude can be illustrated by the problem of identity for concepts and propositions. It is simply not clear when two propositions or concepts are the same. Two propositions or concepts that may seem the same to us can be conjectured to diverge in various possible worlds that can be described. The limits of relevant possibilities are so vague, however, that there seems to be no satisfactory determinate way of settling objectively the question of the identity of two problematic propositions or con-

cepts. This is why philosophers like to find some way
of transferring talk about concepts and propositions to
talk about something that is open to scientific investigation.

In spite of the ontological difficulties with non-
hyphenated views, it seems clear that non-hyphenated
views are required to explain how we can understand belief sentences. The crucial reason why non-hyphenated
views are forced on us is that we have an intuitive feeling for the consistency of belief. So far in this chapter
we have been discussing consciously formulated beliefs,
which are conscious beliefs in the sense of the last
chapter and which are of the sort we would be interested
in incorporating into a rational belief set. It seems obvious that the following pair of assertions of John's
would be regarded as inconsistent:

> (16) I believe that Tom is the best golfer in town.
> (17) I believe that Tom isn't the best golfer in town.

If, instead of (17), John asserts the following,

> (18) I don't believe that Tom is the best golfer in
>   town.

then John could be convicted of inconsistency in terms
of Standard Logic. If John's beliefs expressed in (16)
and (17) are to be regarded as inconsistent, we need to
look within the belief context to find the inconsistency,
and this means that we need some special devices for
dealing with belief contexts that are not provided by
Standard Logic and the hyphenated policy.

An initial approach could be suggested that would
amount to simply comparing the conscious beliefs attributed to John as though they were simple assertions.
Instead of (16) and (17), for example, we could

imagine that John utters (19) and (20), as John might well do in expressing his beliefs to someone over a suitable period of time:

(19) Tom is the best golfer in town.
(20) Tom isn't the best golfer in town.

Using Standard Logic, we can find this pair of sentences to be contradictory. We treat (19) and (20) by this test as though they were exercises in a logic text; that is, as though relevant, normal, semantical presuppositions were satisfied. We assume that there is a person named Tom, that there is a unique town being talked about, and so on. The test is then strictly syntactical. Should various semantical presuppositions not be satisfied, there may not be an outright contradiction. For the time being, we will bring the syntactical tests of Standard Logic to bear on belief sentences and worry about discussing the relevant semantical issues should this strategy prove otherwise profitable.

Summarizing, we take our naïve strategy for dealing with the consistency of belief to be this. If a person utters a number of his beliefs, we can strike off the phrase "I believe that" if it occurs, and test the sentences we get in this fashion by the usual logical methods. Using this device, we find (16) and (17) contradictory because (19) and (20) are regarded as contradictory in context. This naïve strategy will not take us very far. To see this, consider the following schematized belief assertions, where p stands for some declarative sentence:

(21) I believe that p.
(22) I believe that I believe that not p.
(23) I believe that I don't believe that p.

(22) and (23) are quite closely related. (23) is compatible with suspension of belief about p, and (22) is

not, but (22) and (23) might be taken as variants of one another in certain contexts. (21)–(23) supply a cluster of difficulties for the naïve strategy whenever beliefs are iterated in the manner that they represent. Beliefs are said to be iterated when a person has a belief that he does or does not have some other belief. If we apply the first strategy, it only enables us to drop off the outermost belief assertion. Applying the strategy to (21)–(23), for example, we would get these sentences:

    (24) *p.*
    (25) I believe that not *p.*
    (26) I don't believe that *p.*

By the test of Standard Logic, either (24) and (25) or (24) and (26) are consistent. We may, after all, believe what is either true or false. But this generalization holds only if we do not know whether what we believe is true or false, or do not have conflicting beliefs of certain kinds. If a single person were to utter either *pair* of sentences just noted, he is in effect saying that he knowingly believes what is false, or what he believes false. Therefore, either pair of sentences when uttered by a single person seems to involve him in as serious a contradiction as that posed by (16) and (17). The sort of contradiction posed by (24) and (25), or (24) and (26), is known in the literature as *Moore's Paradox.*

The naïve strategy cannot deal with Moore's Paradox in any straightforward way. We might, for example, suggest that *all* of the "I believe that" phrases be deleted before the Standard Logic test of consistency is applied. If we do this, we can reduce (24) and (25) to the following pair of contradictory sentences:

    (27) *p.*
    (28) Not *p.*

But we cannot handle the variant case of (24) and (26) in this fashion since the motivation of the first strategy for dropping "I believe that" will not work for dropping "I don't believe that." To see this, consider this pair of claims:

(29) I don't believe that p.
(30) I don't believe that not p.

Taken together, these claims seem to suggest that the person speaking is agnostic with respect to p, and agnosticism is surely a consistent position in a setting as bare as this. If we follow the strategy of deleting all iterated belief claims, we would turn (29) and (30) into (27) and (28), which are inconsistent. But we cannot in general regard (25) and (26) as equivalent, and it seems dubious that we can have a general method for determining when they can be properly regarded as equivalent in a given context. It appears that we need some more sophisticated strategy for testing consistency than mere deletion of belief phrases.

In order to introduce a more sophisticated strategy, we will develop some symbolism that is widely used in the literature. First, we will consider the set of all facts which agent a either believes, disbelieves, or is agnostic toward. Using the techniques of Sentential Logic, we expose as much truth-functional structure as possible in the set of sentences expressing these facts. ("Fact" is used here merely to describe the kind of state of affairs reported by a factual sentence of the kind we are restricting ourselves to in the analysis. These factual sentences need not be true.) We take the atomic sentence letters which appear as a result of this analysis and consider the set of truth-functional sentential formulae which can be constructed from this set of atomic sentence letters. (We use $\sim$ for negation, $\wedge$ for conjunction, $\lor$ for disjunction, and $\supset$ for the material conditional.) The set of truth-functional sentential formulae will be known as the set of a's *possible beliefs* along with the factual sentences that they abstract. We then introduce six sentential operators, any one of which may be prefixed to a sentential formula from a's possible beliefs, to form a belief sentence or formula abstracting such a sentence. The operators and their readings are given here:

(i) Ba (*a* believes that).
(ii) $\sim Ba$ (*a* doesn't believe that).
(iii) $BaBa$ (*a* believes that *a* believes that).
(iv) $Ba \sim Ba$ (*a* believes that *a* doesn't believe that).
(v) $\sim BaBa$ (*a* doesn't believe that *a* believes that).
(vi) $\sim Ba \sim Ba$ (*a* doesn't believe that *a* doesn't believe that).

We now have a symbolism for representing a's *factual beliefs,* provided that a's belief is not iterated more than twice. This restriction is designed to keep our formalism simple, but as a first approximation it is not a serious restriction. It is difficult to imagine circumstances in which "I believe that I believe that I believe that p" can vary in truth or significance from "I believe that I believe that p." (In many formal treatments of belief, these are taken as provably equivalent because of this fact.) By prefixing one of the belief operators to a possible belief, we can represent those beliefs of a that concern us.

In testing beliefs for consistency, we start with the set of formulae (prefixed with one of the operators) each member of which represents one of a's conscious beliefs in the circumstances. Call this set of formulae the set of a's *distinguished beliefs.* The distinguished belief set is always finite. In testing *a*'s distinguished beliefs for consistency, we will regard ourselves as free to use Sentential Logic in any way that will prove helpful. The test for consistency is to develop a set of *model belief sets* from the set of *a*'s distinguished beliefs, which represent the possible ways in which *a*'s beliefs might all be true compatibly with various facts and the set of *a*'s beliefs themselves. If there is no such possible way, then *a*'s distinguished belief set is inconsistent.

The first step of development will be called Belief Augmentation. All formulae that can be obtained from formulae in *a*'s distinguished belief set by deleting the prefix *Ba*, or by changing the prefix *Ba* $\sim Ba$ to $\sim Ba$, or by *both* changing the prefix *BaBa* to *Ba and* deleting it altogether (thus adding two formulae if neither of the resulting formulae are already in the set), are added to the formulae in *a*'s distinguished belief set. We call *a*'s distinguished belief set *B*. Call the set obtained by Belief Augmentation the set *B**. If *B** is inconsistent by Sentential Logic, then *B* is inconsistent.[2] The Sentential Logic test of consistency amounts to determining whether *B* can be incorporated into an infinite set (closed under the operation of logical consequence in Sentential Logic) that is consistent. For example, let *B* = {*Bap, Ba~p*}. Then *B** = {*Bap, Ba~p, p, ~p*}, which is manifestly inconsistent by Sentential Logic. Therefore *B* is inconsistent. This shows that (19) and (20) can be accommodated by our methods. Our intuitive motivation for developing *B** is nearly obvious; *a*'s beliefs are intuitively consistent only if they could all be true. Belief Augmentation is the formal way of supposing that they are all true.

---

[2] Technical note. This requires a trivial revision of the rules of Sentential Logic to count formulae with one of the prefixes attached as abstracting a distinct sentence.

Suppose that $B*$ is consistent for some distinguished belief set B belonging to a. Consider formulae of the sort that has an abstracted prefix $\sim Ba$. Each such formula abstracts a sentence asserting that a does not believe something. Because of the possibility of agnosticism, this could happen if a believes the denial of whatever comes after the prefix, or if a believes that the denial of whatever comes after the prefix is compatible with everything else that he believes. But a's claim in either event is inconsistent with the beliefs given in $B*$ if the denial of what comes after the prefix is inconsistent with the abstracted sentences in $B*$. For example, if $\sim Bap$ is in $B*$, then a's not believing that p is consistent with the sentences in $B*$ only if no inconsistency results from adding $\sim p$ to $B*$. In this case, a is free to believe $\sim p$ if he cares to. But if there is an inconsistency, he is not free to believe $\sim p$ because p is a logical consequence of his positive beliefs. Each sentence with the prefix $\sim Ba$ can thus be tested for consistency by adding the denial of the sentence filling in the blank to $B*$ and testing the resulting set for consistency. We will say that the Disbelief Procedure is applied to $B*$ if the denial of the sentence coming after some prefix $\sim Ba$ is added to $B*$. If there are n formulae with the prefix $\sim Ba$ in the set $B*$, the Disbelief Procedure can be applied n times to obtain n different possible model sets for B from $B*$. Call these possible model sets B_1*, $B_2* \ldots B_n*$. Each of these sets must be consistent if B is to be consistent. To test for consistency, we apply Belief Augmentation to each set B_i so as to obtain a set B_i* in which all formulae that can be obtained from B_i by Belief Augmentation are found as members. The resulting set B_i* is then tested for consistency using the methods of Standard Logic. Obviously, each set B_i^* must be consistent if B is to be regarded as consistent.

We now take some examples. First, let $B = \{\sim Bap, \sim Ba\sim p\}$. Applying the procedure discussed in the last paragraph, we get $B_1^* = \{\sim Bap, \sim Ba\sim p, \sim p\}$, and $B_2^* = \{\sim Bap, \sim Ba\sim p, \sim\sim p\}$. Both B_1^* and B_2^* are consistent by Standard Logic, so B is consistent. This result is compatible with intuition since this is the simplest case in which a pair of expressed beliefs represent agnosticism with respect to some assertion.

When we form the belief sets $B_1^*, B_2^* \ldots B_n^*$, the reason why we add but one non-belief at a time to what the agent believes is that it is perfectly acceptable for an agent *not* to believe each sentence of a pair of sentences which together are contradictory. The simplest case of agnosticism is sufficient to show that if we add two sentences not believed by an agent (whose beliefs are consistent) to the set B^*, we may get a contradiction.

Our procedure can easily be extended to handle some more difficult cases. We consider two such cases here. Suppose a says "I believe both that p and that I don't believe that p." (This is a variant of Moore's Paradox.) This could be abstracted to $B = \{Bap, Ba\sim Bap\}$ and easily shown inconsistent by our method. The reader should verify that Moore's Paradox is shown inconsistent in previous versions by considering (24) and (25), (24) and (26) in the light of our test for consistency. At the same time, given the natural interpretation of the prefix Ba, we could utilize a mixture of Sentential Logic and the property of our belief operators that they turn sentences into sentences to abstract Moore's Paradox for a as follows:

$$Ba(p \wedge \sim Bap).$$

This abstracts the claim that *a* believes both that *p* and that *Bap*. This is easily shown inconsistent by an obvious and trivial extension of our method.

We could also introduce the beliefs of others by means of such operators as *Bb, Bc,* etc. Suppose *a* believes that a pair of *b*'s beliefs involve Moore's Paradox. This situation might be abstracted by the following pair of formulae:

(i)   *BaBbp.*
(ii) *BaBb ~Bbp.*

In using Belief Augmentation and the Disbelief Procedure, we apply them *only* to the agent whose beliefs are being considered. We have $B = \{BaBbp, BaBb{\sim}Bbp\}$ and $B^* = \{BaBbp, BaBb{\sim}Bbp, Bbp, Bb{\sim}Bbp\}$. B^* is not inconsistent by Sentential Logic. So our augmented test allows *a* to be consistent if he believes *b* to be inconsistent, and this is the correct intuitive result. The last two paragraphs indicate how Belief Augmentation and the Disbelief Procedure can be utilized to obtain more powerful tests of consistency.

The test we have sketched here will stand as our test for the consistency of belief. Intuitively, this test examines whether a man's beliefs are consistent by testing whether the total set of his beliefs is consistent with the truth of what he believes as well as the fact that he has the beliefs that he does. This test is a sufficient test for inconsistency, but it is not a complete test of consistency for a reason that is related to the reason why the Sentential Logic test of consistency is not sufficient for logical consistency in general. A given set of sentences may be consistent under the test of Sentential Logic (in which logic it is assumed that different sentences are independent) yet be inconsistent in the test of Predicate Logic where various kinds of dependency can be formalized which are not captured by the notion of logical form used in Sentential Logic. What is true is that if a set of sentences is inconsistent by the test of Sentential Logic, then it is also inconsistent by the test of Predicate Logic. Sometimes, however, a set of sentences consistent in Sentential Logic can be shown inconsistent in Predicate Logic when more sophisticated dependencies of form are exhibited. An obvious move for increasing the sophistication of our test for the consistency of belief is to use the belief prefixes that we have used, but to allow the logical form of the sentences filling the blanks to be expressed by the formulae of Predicate Logic. Then, using the more sophisticated methods of Predicate Logic (perhaps with identity), we can test sets of sentences for consistency and find some inconsistencies which would escape the test introduced in this chapter. This development is explored in the more advanced treatises mentioned in the Further Reading section. The use of Predicate Logic introduces a number of very serious problems, not all of which have been resolved. These are introduced very briefly in the Appendix, which the interested reader should consult.

Chapter 3

Rational Belief

In the previous chapter, we considered a person's beliefs as given, and we considered a simple model for testing the consistency of such a set of beliefs by determining whether it could be incorporated into an infinite set of sentences that were logically consistent. Consistent rational belief, however, even consistent rational belief in our defined sense, may seem only a partial criterion for what is known intuitively as rational belief. We can easily suppose the beliefs of a lunatic to be logically consistent and incorporable into a rational belief set in our defined sense, so that lunacy is not a matter of inconsistency, but a matter of interpreting available information in some arbitrarily strange way. In addition to logical consistency, which is simply a deepened form of a familiar notion, there are some other relevant considerations that can be applied to sets of beliefs. Let us suppose that some person numbers among his beliefs both the belief that there is life on Mars and the belief that John Adams was once President of the United States. It is easy to imagine circumstances in which we would say that he believes the latter more strongly than he does the former. For example, he might be quite willing to bet "at any odds" against anyone holding the claim that while John Adams was an important American founding father, he never achieved the office of President. (We'll assume that there is no potential confusion about which John Adams is under discussion.) The claim can be quickly settled by checking with a reference book or two. At the same time, he might not be willing to bet about life on Mars. His reasons for this could be complex. The belief is somewhat vague— for discovery of an unanticipated kind by a future space flight might result in an argument about who had won the bet. One reason for this is the relatively unclear criteria for life in general, which makes it difficult to decide whether such cases as various viral particles are alive, and so forth. Let us suppose that this person disagrees with someone about whether there is life on Mars, but that the two agree that certain results of a planned space flight would resolve the issue. Then a bet might be made at certain fixed odds. Given a reasonable projected scenario, it seems that the total information at our agent's disposal is apt to make it much more likely that John Adams was once President than that there is life on Mars. Then the agent could easily be seen to rationally prefer a bet "even up" on the Presidency of John Adams to a bet "even up" on a favorable outcome to the space flight. This situation and the related intuition yields a clue that can be utilized to extend consistency of belief into a notion about rationality.

We will assume here that what counts as evidence for or against a given belief can be objectively determined. If I believe that a given coin is fair, and then discover in tossing it one hundred times that I get ninety-five heads, this counts as evidence against my belief. As far as logical consistency is concerned, however, I can believe that the coin is fair even though the only relevant evidence is against this belief. Most people grasping the situation would probably regard my continuing to hold that the coin was fair in the light of this evidence rather suspect, if not downright irrational. The clue mentioned in the last paragraph is then taken in the following way. If my beliefs are to be regarded as rational, not only must they be logically consistent, they must also be related to the evidence I have at my command in such a fashion that beliefs which are rendered highly unlikely on that evidence are not believed by me. Our clue thus leads to the following more comprehensive definition of a rational belief set. A rational belief set is a consistent set of beliefs such that the person holding this set does not hold equally strongly two beliefs which are quite different in likelihood given the evidence at his command, and such that the person does not hold one belief much more strongly than another when the evidence at his command renders them equally likely or suggests that the latter is more likely than the former.

This definition seems to handle some outstanding cases of lunacy pretty well. A man (presumed to be an obvious lunatic) who believes very strongly that his brother is trying to poison him (in spite of appearances) and who believes, rather weakly by comparison, that Boston is north of New York is likely to be flying in the face of the evidence and the claims that the evidence renders likely. It seems promising to conjecture that if we can work out the details of an evidential or likelihood relationship using probability theory, we could define a rational belief set as a logically consistent belief set in which strengths of belief are assigned relative to evidence in a way that does not conflict with our own notions of what is evidence for and against a belief.

The first clarification that must be effected is a more detailed consideration of what is to count as the available evidence for assessing the rationality of a belief set. We have spoken of the evidence available to a person, but this is subject to an interpretation that would leave our definition of rationality quite compatible with lunacy. A lunatic who is interested just in those beliefs that make him crazy might also single-mindedly notice and accumulate evidence relevant only to those beliefs. Then his crazy beliefs will be as likely as any beliefs he has relative to the evidence of which he has taken note. Even the lunatic will have been exposed to evidence that would render other beliefs more likely than the beliefs that stamp him as deviant from norms of rationality. In order to circumvent this, some commentators have required that a rational agent consider the likelihood of his beliefs relative to the total evidence available to him at any time. A requirement of total evidence quite obviously removes us to a plane of idealization similar to that attained by requiring that a rational belief set be closed under deductive consequence, provided that the requirement of total evidence is a clear notion. It is not easy to see how to exclude the results of experiments that might *easily* be done from available evidence, or even the results of experiments that have been done but have gone unreported, or have been reported in another language. Study of these and related problems indicates that the exact nature of the concept of total available evidence is not clear. We will have to make do with a fairly intuitive notion. A rational belief set must be assessed relative to evidence that is a somewhat idealized extension of what an honest and open-minded inquirer might have available to him at the time his belief set is assessed. Given the correctness of the view that our beliefs in part determine the nature of the evidence available to us, this means that the same total evidence is not available to all honest inquirers, and we need to depend on the notion that there will be a considerable overlap of evidence to help to force similar estimates of various controversial beliefs. This is a rather makeshift notion, but fortunately it turns out that the important difficulties with the notion of rational belief are not to be traced primarily to a vague concept of evidence. The makeshift idea suggests that there should be a considerable overlap between the evidence used by two different rational agents to assess their belief sets when these agents are assessing their beliefs under circumstances in which they are close to one another in time and share similar scientific backgrounds. Perhaps we can make no stronger assumption compatibly with an adequate epistemology for science.

Now let us consider a set of beliefs and attempt to define more precisely when a set of beliefs is rational. We will assume once again that the beliefs are held sufficiently simultaneously so as not to change in content while they are assessed, and we will assume that the likelihood of the beliefs is to be assessed against a fixed set of evidential sentences. A first necessary condition for rationality will be consistency of the sort discussed in Chapter 6. The second necessary condition for rationality will be that strengths of beliefs be assigned compatibly with the probability calculus. We need to digress for a moment to discuss this requirement.

Our original intuition in this chapter was that some beliefs are held more strongly than others. This suggests that it should be possible to compare any two beliefs and decide which is stronger. While it suggests this, it really does not force this as a consequence, so we need to make it an assumption or make some other assumption which has this as a consequence. For beliefs which are sufficiently vague, or for beliefs which have very high or very low probabilities, a person may feel that precise comparison with sharp beliefs is precluded. In order to circumvent a long and diffuse discussion, we will assume that sufficient thought could enable us to tell of any two beliefs, whether we hold them equally strongly or hold one of them more strongly than the other, at least to a degree of precision that would result in a workable theory utilizing the probability calculus.

Suppose we start with someone's set of conscious beliefs. As in the last chapter, we will assume that this set is finite, although it may be very large. Let us assume that this set of beliefs is consistent as shown by the test introduced in the last chapter. Suppose agent a believes p and believes q, and that p and q are in his set of possible beliefs as a result. Bap and Baq abstract the fact that he holds these beliefs, but a is not interested in comparing the strength of these two sentences. They are both simply true. He may well be interested in comparing the strength with which he believes p with the strength with which he believes q. The strength with which he holds these beliefs measures, in a sense, his feeling that he might have to give up the belief in the face of adverse evidence. Strength therefore appears to him as a property of p and q with respect to the available evidence and the expected future evidence. The numbers to be assigned to p and q indicate a's view as to the relative likelihood of p and q given all that he believes. These numbers do depend on the agent a or on some property of the agent (possibly the language that he speaks), but we will assign numbers without indexing them with a's name, simply keeping in mind, from the context, the job that the numbers are supposed to do. First, we will assume that a assigns numbers to all his conscious beliefs which are in his set of possible beliefs, assigning the strongest thing that he believes the value 1 and weaker beliefs real numbers in the interval $(0, 1)$.

Consider the set of a's possible beliefs. As numbers are assigned to his conscious beliefs, probability theory places a number of constraints on the assignment he may make to the set of his possible beliefs. Let p be one of his actual beliefs. Both p and $\sim p$ will be in the set of his possible beliefs. By probability theory, if p is assigned the number x in the interval $(0, 1)$, then $\sim p$ must be assigned the number $1-x$. Again, probability theory requires that if p and q are independent (may be true or false independently), then if p is assigned x and q is assigned y, we must have it that $p \vee q$ is assigned $x + y$ and $p \wedge q$ is assigned $x \times y$. This information is sufficient to indicate the constraints that probability theory puts on a set of formulae which are truth-functions of some finite set of atomic formulae as in the case of a's possible beliefs. For this simplified case, then, the constraints imposed by probability theory are easy to grasp. Any consistent set of possible beliefs can be given an assignment of numbers which is compatible with the constraints of probability theory. Let p_1, p_2 . . . p_n be the atomic formulae of a's set of possible beliefs. Then the number $1/n$ can be assigned to each of the p_i and numbers for the truth-functions of these formulae can be assigned according to the instructions given above. We call any assignment of real numbers in the interval $(0, 1)$ to a's set of possible beliefs which satisfies the constraints of probability theory a *coherent belief assignment*.

A coherent belief assignment is still not necessarily an assignment of numbers representing the relative strengths of rational belief. The reason for this is that the numbers assigned to the beliefs in such a coherent belief assignment may satisfy the constraints of probability theory and still not be assigned in accordance with the intuitive likelihoods of the beliefs given the available evidence. To achieve this desideratum, we must also require that if one belief is more likely than another, given the available evidence, then the former is assigned a number that is higher than the number assigned to the latter. When this condition is met, we will refer to a coherent belief assignment as a rational ordered belief set. If we could make the notion of the likelihood of a given belief on the available evidence and of the available evidence itself both clear, the notion of a rational ordered belief set seems to capture the intuitions about rationality that we have previously discussed.

Let us return for a moment to the concept of rationality itself. If a man's set of actual belief sentences is consistent, and if its related set of possible beliefs can be incorporated into a rational ordered belief set, we will tentatively say that the man is rational. There is one consequence of our assignment of numbers to beliefs in the rational ordered belief set that should be explicitly noticed. By the consistency requirement, we can't have both a sentence and its negation in the set of a person's actual beliefs. When we incorporate a set of actual beliefs into a rational ordered belief set preserving a likelihood ordering, therefore, we must not assign a real number less than or equal to .5 to any actual belief, say p. In such an event, $\sim p$ would be assigned a real number greater than that assigned to p, so p would be believed even though $\sim p$ had a greater likelihood on the available evidence. This situation violates the intuition underlying the assignment of likelihood numbers. Therefore, we will require that a person's actual beliefs all be assigned a value greater than .5 in his rational ordered belief set. This will prevent the situation just noted from arising. The consistency of actual belief is tested by closure under logical consequence. If our agent discovers that something is a logical consequence of his actual beliefs, he must then also assign that consequence a value greater than .5 in his rational ordered belief set. All of the logical consequences of the agent's actual conscious beliefs which can be expressed in terms of truth-functions of his simplest beliefs will be in his set of possible beliefs. In attempting to fit consistency with likelihood as criteria of rationality, then, we must require that all logical consequences of actual conscious beliefs in an agent's possible belief set be assigned a value greater than .5.

We have now set the stage for an intriguing puzzle. Although each step of argument about rational belief and the intuitions involved seem reasonable, we have now placed restrictions on rational belief which are so strong that they cannot be jointly satisfied in many interesting cases. Such a representative case is that given by the so-called lottery paradox. Suppose three slips of paper are marked with the numerals 1, 2, and 3 and are thoroughly mixed in a hat. One of the slips is to be drawn from the hat by a child. A person knowing the details of the lottery may regard it as fair, that is, he may regard it as equally likely that any of the slips will be drawn. Let's examine the beliefs of such a person, on the assumption of intuitive rationality. He probably believes that slip 1 will not be drawn, since the probability of this slip being drawn is ⅓ on a simple probability model. A similar situation exists for the other slips. We can summarize this in the following fashion. Let $\sim S1$, $\sim S2$, $\sim S3$ abstract the three sentences each expressing a claim that one of the slips will not be drawn. These sentences will all be in the belief set of the person involved. So will be the sentence abstracted to $S1 \lor S2 \lor S3$, which abstracts a sentence expressing the belief that one of the slips will be drawn. The agent's beliefs are consistent so far. But by deductive closure, the agent cannot disbelieve the sentence abstracted to $\sim S1 \land \sim S2 \land \sim S3$, for this sentence follows from those expressing his beliefs about the individual slips not being drawn. This sentence, however, expresses a claim that no slip will be drawn, contradicting the expressed belief that some slip will be drawn. The agent regards $S1 \lor S2 \lor S3$ as a certainty. He therefore (let us say) assigns it a value of 1. All of $\sim S1$, $\sim S2$, and $\sim S3$ have a value greater than .5. So $\sim S1 \land \sim S2 \land \sim S3$ must have a value greater than .5 since it is a logical consequence of $\sim S1$, $\sim S2$, and $\sim S3$. But $\sim S1 \land \sim S2 \land \sim S3$ is the denial of $S1 \lor S2 \lor S3$ in this context. Hence, if $S1 \lor S2 \lor S3$ is assigned a value greater than .5, the probability constraints require that $\sim S1 \land \sim S2 \land \sim S3$ be assigned a value less than .5, contrary to our rationality requirement that it also be assigned a value greater than .5.

The lottery paradox raises a serious difficulty for the analysis of rational belief that we have been pursuing to this point. Apparently, we must abandon one or more of the assumptions that we have been making along the way. Among these assumptions are the following. In the first place, we accepted the intuition provided by ordinary language that there are some things a person believes, and that there are some things he disbelieves, and that there are some things he is agnostic about. We can call this the detachment assumption. This assumption leads us to accept the view that a person has a set of conscious beliefs which he recognizes, and from which he draws various inferences in the course of planning his rational activities. Another assumption was the deductivity assumption to the effect that a rational man cannot rationally choose to disbelieve or be agnostic about any deductive consequence of what he believes. The third assumption we will call the likelihood assumption. This assumption is not independent of the first. In effect, it suggests that a rational man will believe all propositions whose likelihood in the face of total evidence is greater than some fixed number. (We have seen that it must be greater than .5.) Various strategies for avoiding the difficulties hinted at in the lottery paradox amount to relaxing one or more of these assumptions. We will describe briefly how various philosophers have relaxed one or two of these assumptions and produced consistent accounts of rational belief that seem at the same time to violate some of the intuitions of other philosophers who have chosen to weaken some other assumption. At the present time, the situation is this. One can avoid the lottery paradox by producing an account of belief that seems only partial and satisfies only some of the intuitions that were invoked in leading to the paradox. What this means is that one can satisfy one of these accounts, or that an idealized agent could satisfy one of these accounts, and still appear to be irrational to at least some philosophers on the basis of quite plausible intuitions. Whether this situation can be resolved is a matter of quite interesting current philosophical research.

One obvious strategy for defeating the lottery paradox is to give up the deductivity assumption. Then a person may have detached beliefs, and it can be required that they be ordered according to the likelihood assumption; what is not required is that a person or idealized agent believe every logical consequence of what he believes. A vestige of consistency may nonetheless remain. Inconsistency can be defined as a person's holding a *pair* of beliefs that would be abstracted to formulae like $Ba\phi$ and $Ba{\sim}\phi$, for some formula ϕ. It may now be required that a person's beliefs be closed under logical consequence in the sense that every logical consequence of each single belief that he has be included in his set of idealized conscious beliefs. If $Ba(p\wedge{\sim}p)$ is true of a, then so are Bap and $Ba{\sim}p$ by this requirement, so a is inconsistent. What is excluded is the following. If Bap and Baq abstract beliefs of a, it does not follow that a must have a belief abstracted to $Ba(p\wedge q)$ in order to be rational. This avoids the lottery paradox since the agent need not believe ${\sim}S1 \wedge {\sim}S2 \wedge {\sim}S3$ because he believes ${\sim}S1$, ${\sim}S2$, and ${\sim}S3$. This strategy has proved repugnant to most philosophers whose intuitions have required that if a person has any detached beliefs, rationality requires that they be closed under logical consequence.

It is clear that the deductivity assumption and the detachment assumption are related. If there are no detached beliefs, deduction of beliefs from beliefs is not in question. A second strategy for dealing with the lottery paradox involves giving up the detachment assumption altogether. Let us return to the agent's belief that the slip with the numeral 1 on it will not be drawn. ${\sim}S1$ was used to abstract the agent's detached belief. The belief in question may be regarded as more precise than that, however. A person might detach belief that the slip will not be drawn because he believes that it had never been put into the hat, or that it had been destroyed. In such a case, his belief that the slip would not be drawn would be categorical in the sense that he would give no credence to the belief that the slip might be drawn. Given the circumstances of the lottery, however, he would not be amazed if the slip were drawn, although he might be surprised in view of the odds against it. Perhaps the agent's belief is thus better put

in some such way as the following: The probability of
the slip with the numeral 1 on it not being drawn is $\frac{2}{3}$.
Let us represent this as $p(\sim S1) = \frac{2}{3}$. The total beliefs
about the lottery which an agent using the suggested
probability model would have can then be set down
as follows:

$$p(S1) = \frac{1}{3}.$$
$$p(S2) = \frac{1}{3}.$$
$$p(S3) = \frac{1}{3}.$$
$$p(\sim S1) = p(S2 \vee S3) = \frac{2}{3}.$$
$$p(\sim S2) = p(S1 \vee S3) = \frac{2}{3}.$$
$$p(\sim S3) = p(S1 \vee S2) = \frac{2}{3}.$$
$$p(S1 \vee S2 \vee S3) = 1.$$
$$p(\sim S1 \wedge \sim S2 \wedge \sim S3) = 0.$$

These formulae abstract beliefs are all consistent with
the constraints imposed by probability theory. In this
situation, the agent does not believe $\sim S1$ and disbelieve $S2$, but his beliefs are construed as a weighing of
the possible events according to the likelihood of their
happening according to a simple probability model.
There is no detachment of belief and hence no problem about the logical consequences of detached beliefs.
None of these beliefs is a *logical consequence* of any
other. Under this construal no inconsistency exists, and
the lottery paradox has vanished. We will call this theory—that beliefs should always be regarded as probability assignments—the theory of *partial belief*. On this
view, a person has few, if any, detached beliefs. Rather,
he weighs various likelihoods against one another according to the consequences of a consistent probability
model of possible events.

On partial belief theories, the detachment assumption is rejected (save possibly for the detachment of a
few special beliefs), and the deductivity assumption is

retained only in the guise that compatibility with the probability calculus requires that if ϕ is a logical consequence of ψ, then the likelihood assignment to ϕ must be at least as high as the assignment to ψ. It is also clear that the likelihood assumption is not accepted in its usual form. This is one reason why so many philosophers have found partial belief theories to be unsatisfactory. Our earlier example of the man with a psychotic fear that his brother was trying to poison him is sufficient to indicate why this is the case. Objections of this kind can be met by partial belief theories that do contain a modified likelihood assumption. On these theories, some further constraints than those imposed by probability theory are imposed on the probability assignments permitted by the theory. Such a likelihood assumption can work as follows. From a's possible beliefs, consider first the set of atomic formulae. A probability assignment satisfying certain a priori desiderata is made to these sentences, and the probability assignments to the rest of the formulae are then calculated according to the constraints imposed by probability theory. In our example, it was clear that equal assignments to all of the atomic formulae was the correct intuitive assignment, but this is not always right. Any assignment such that the sum of the assignments to the atomic formulae equals 1 will satisfy the probability calculus. The objections to available likelihood programs center on the fact that suitable a priori constraints for reasonable assignments of likelihood do not exist in all cases where a set of possible beliefs is expressed in terms of logical structure more complicated than that which can be expressed using Sentential Logic.

A general objection to all theories of partial belief is that they obscure the connection between belief and action. Partial belief requires the rational agent to assign numbers to sentences to represent their likelihood, and other numbers to the same sentences (here we can only allude to this) to represent the desirability or utility of the state of affairs described in the sentence to the agent. The agent then calculates the various *expected* utilities of the acts available to him, and then he performs that action (if he is rational) with as high an expected utility as is available. The word "expected" indicates how probabilities are involved. The expected utility of an act is the sum of all the utilities that might accrue from its performance, each multiplied by the probability that the act will produce that utility. An act very likely to bring about disaster but offering a slim chance for ecstasy will not have higher expected utility than an act offering a fairly high probability of bringing about either of two very desirable outcomes. (The details depend on the exact numerical likelihood and utility assignments.) While we often act in the face of a perceived uncertainty (where the partial belief theory fits the situation and our intuitions about it), we also act quite frequently because we think that so-and-so will happen even though we know that the facts do not force this view on us, and we might be flying in the face of a reasonable probability model. In other words, we often take a view about things and act on our view, a procedure that suggests that we do detach certain beliefs and act on them as though they were true even though we could not rationally assign them a probability of 1, or even a very high probability. It might even be the case that an adequate psychology will support this view in that humans may find it most convenient not to assign weights to a set of possible beliefs in every case, but to adopt certain beliefs as a model of the world and act on these beliefs until they run into difficulty, at which time various possible revisions can be formulated and examined. Should this be the case, partial belief theories would only be partial theories that were explanatory of human behavior under circumstances where a high degree of uncertainty about the future is explicitly recognized as an important feature of a decision problem.

To a person with no prior commitment, the argument about partial belief theories and their adequacy is somewhat inconclusive. Theoretical elegance lies on the side of partial belief. Against it are opposed strong intuitions that suggest the view that it is an incomplete model of rationality. This issue can be partly resolved by remembering our restrictions, particularly our restriction to factual beliefs. Where factual beliefs only are involved, partial belief theories offer a theoretically elegant account of belief structures that are no doubt adequate for philosophical analysis of scientific and business decision making. Unfortunately, the account breaks down for aesthetic, ethical, and political beliefs, or for decisions where such beliefs themselves may be questioned. It simply does not survive scrutiny, for example, to talk about the probability of an obligation to do something. Here beliefs are likely to be detached, that is, the agent is likely to believe that he definitely ought or ought not to do some action when all of the relevant moral considerations have been examined. Probability can refer only to an estimate of which is really the case, and here we can sharply distinguish the probability of an estimate from the facts of the case which would, if fully known, rule out one of the alternatives. Some moral problems may depend on a perception of the future as undetermined, but many do not, and in these latter cases the probability of having an obligation is simply not applicable. For many ordinary purposes, we do take positive views and act on their consequences, perhaps as a result of explicit or implicit practical reasoning about these detached beliefs. For these situations, the partial belief theories cannot offer an adequate account of rational belief that can be coupled with reasonable views about practical deliberation and action.

The third and last strategy to be mentioned here for defeating the lottery paradox involves keeping the detachment and deductivity assumptions (along with coherent belief assignments as a test of consistency where applicable) and rejecting the likelihood assumption. An intuitive motivation for this strategy is provided by many betting situations. Suppose we can bet "even up" with someone on the outcome of drawing a card at random from a randomly shuffled deck of cards. In the first case, we can bet either that the card drawn will be a spade, or that it will be the king of hearts. If neither a spade nor the heart king is drawn, the bet is off. The bet to take is obvious, given the situation. Now the likelihood of drawing a spade on the intuitive probability model is only one in four, so our chances of winning money on the bet are not good. The reason for making the bet is that the chance of getting a spade is high relative to the alternative, drawing the king of hearts. What this shows is that the attractiveness of a possibility is a function of the alternatives to it. In a second case similar to the first, if we could bet either that the card drawn will be a spade, or that it will be either a heart or diamond, we would clearly choose not to bet on a spade being drawn. What these examples suggest is this. When we have some sort of problem (scientific or otherwise) we often approach it with a fixed set of possible solutions from which we are to choose an answer. What we look for is not high likelihood in an answer *per se,* but a sufficiently higher likelihood of an answer than that possessed by any of the relevant alternatives.

These insights can be turned into a strategy that defeats the lottery paradox. The procedure for belief then looks like this. If we have an exhaustive set of possible solutions to some problem, and our information (which seems not to be biased and is reasonably comprehensive) entails that one of the possible solutions has a much greater likelihood of being true on the information than any of the alternative solutions, then we accept that solution (believe it to be true and detach it) along with all of its deductive consequences, and we refuse to believe any of the other alternative solutions. Let's look at the lottery paradox with this in mind. The set of alternative solutions to the outcome of the lottery is: $S1$, $S2$, and $S3$. Since the lottery is fair, our information entails that the likelihood of any ticket winning is the same as that for any other ticket. We therefore do not detach *any* of $S1$, $S2$, or $S3$, and we suspend belief in the outcome. This is in accordance with intuition. Note that although $S2 \lor S3$ has a higher likelihood than $S1$, we do not detach $S2 \lor S3$ because it is not an alternative to $S1$ in the original set of solutions. Suppose, however, that one has an opportunity to bet on the ticket marked with the numeral 1, but not on the tickets marked with the other numerals, and one can only bet "even up." Now the likelihood of $S1$ is to be compared to the likelihood of $S2 \lor S3$. The set of solutions to this betting problem is the following: $S1$, $S2 \lor S3$. Here one can accept $S2 \lor S3$ and, consequently, refuse to believe $S1$ as well as refusing the bet. It is clear that this third strategy can handle the lottery paradox satisfactorily.

Objections to the third strategy center around two kinds of arguments. The first is that the *scientist* does want high likelihood of his theories being true before he accepts them. A sufficient rejoinder is that scientists, like ordinary people, are often *forced* to take a view about things under pressure of relieving a bad situation before some sort of deadline. In other words, scientists cannot always afford to wait to be sure that their conjectures are correct. Likelihood theorists and partial belief theorists have defended a view that such scientists are not pure scientists, but are best regarded as engineers or technicians of some kind. This seems to be an uninteresting semantic quibble in the sense that a theory of belief seems in order for this activity, whether it be called science or engineering or anything that one pleases. A much more penetrating objection is related to the nature of possible sets of alternative solutions and the way in which they come to be formulated. It is clear that solutions to various belief problems are highly sensitive to the choice of a set of solutions. Since a man may choose problems and solution sets under no constraints imposed by the theory except that the solution set *exhaust* possible answers to the problem, this theory as stated is as permissive in a sense as partial belief theories without a likelihood assumption, and it is possible to describe examples of belief detachment allowed by the theory which violate intuitions about rationality. Two theorists may divide the possible solutions in different ways, thus leading them to make different choices of solution from solution sets that are actually equivalent. It also seems clear that this theory is very local in its outlook, defining a belief procedure only for particular problems and their solutions. This local feature is somewhat at odds with philosophical desiderata for a full theory of rationality, since it is not clear that a man working simultaneously on several problems can be regarded as having one master problem and a solution set for it that would define a sense of rationality for all of the beliefs he might accept over a short period of time.

In these first three chapters, we have found that there is no completely satisfactory philosophical analysis of rational belief. Even when strong restrictions are placed on the kinds of belief to be analyzed, it turns out that *all* of the seemingly reasonable assumptions about rationality that have been proposed cannot be simultaneously satisfied without entailing severe difficulties. The lottery paradox is a good example of the kind of severe difficulty that is encountered, and we have developed our account by discussing this paradox in one particular form in some detail. We have seen how various strategies can be employed to relax one or more of the assumptions leading to the paradox so as to find a consistent account of rationality. All of these accounts are only partial. In suitable circumstances about belief, they seem to provide sound necessary conditions for rationality. But in each case it is possible to describe counterexamples in which the theory is satisfied, but in which the agent involved does not seem to be fully rational according to philosophical idealization. It is quite clear, therefore, that the problem of finding a sound philosophical account of consistent rational belief is likely to be an active area of philosophical investigation for some time to come.

Chapter 4

Kinds of Knowledge

Our discussion of belief in the first three chapters should have prepared the reader for thinking about restrictions on knowledge that may be required before analysis can yield any interesting results. A restriction that was imposed on belief to yield results was to limit belief to factual belief. In a similar way, philosophical analysis of knowledge has been directed almost entirely to factual knowledge. The significance of this restriction is somewhat different in the two cases, and this is reflected by differences in the grammar of the relevant words used to express various states of belief and knowledge in human beings.

The use of formulae like *Bap* to abstract sentences like *"a* believes that *p"* is perspicuous given the restriction to factual belief. There are, however, other grammatical constructions associated with belief sentences in English that require some discussion. The three important cases can be presented by these examples:

(1) *a* believes in God.
(2) *a* believes the theory of evolution.
(3) *a* believes what his mother tells him.

Philosophers are generally agreed that all such cases can be found in context to be equivalent to other sentences using the familiar *"a* believes that*"* prefixed

to some factual sentence. Given the right contexts,
(1)–(3) might be rephrasable as follows:

(4) *a* believes that God is as Martin Luther describes
     Him.

(5) *a* believes that the theory of evolution provides
     the correct account of the development of life
     on earth.

(6) *a* believes that everything his mother says is true.

Although this kind of reduction is generally assumed
by philosophers to be possible, there are a few aspects
of such reduction that are worth noticing.

From a grammatical point of view, *believes* can be
replaced by *knows* in (2) and (3) but not in (1). We
do not have the prefix "*a* knows in," which results in
a knowledge claim when prefixed to a sentence. This
fact can be explained as a result of an important relationship between belief and knowledge. *We can believe
some things that we cannot know.* This situation can
come about in at least two ways. The deeper case exists
whenever I can formulate some claim and believe it to
be true, but circumstances prevent me from knowing
it to be true. For example, *a* may believe that no crea-
tures exist anywhere in the universe except on earth
with which he could mate, but he could not know this.
This kind of case gives rise to a second case in which
a belief is possible, but knowledge is impossible. (The
following example is due to Ronald DeSousa of the
University of Toronto.) An agent may *believe* that
God exists, and that he is in no position to know that
God exists, but he could not *know* the same complex
claim. The grammatical case we have been considering seems an instance of a kind of case in which we ex-
ploit recognition of beliefs that cannot be known.
Typically, the case may involve a belief about something
relatively indeterminate, so that one may believe that

all the consequences or properties of something will be thus-and-so, but one cannot know this because they are infinite in number, or indeterminate in some sense. God's properties are presumed unknowable against this background, and this fact seems reflected in the grammatical situation. Believing *in* things seems to be a useful construction for describing various kinds of unknowable or indeterminate beliefs. At first glance, this may seem violated by constructions in which a person believes *in doing* something, but here, typically, the agent believes in doing something in order to guard against various possibilities in an indeterminate future. One may believe in keeping his car locked. Why? Because one never knows what will happen, as we say. Cases of this latter sort, however, have been excluded by the restriction to factual belief. All of the foregoing is quite compatible with holding that *believing in* constructions (where factual) can fit the model of believing that something is the case through the careful use of contextual analysis of meaning. Contextual analysis usually shifts the indeterminacy into the clause from the *believing in* construction. (4), for example, does not describe the properties that God has, or enumerate them, it merely alludes to a characterization of them that could not easily be summarized. This reflects the indeterminacy of the belief claimed in (1).

The same fact that we can believe what we cannot know is important to the constructions in (2) and (3). Although *believes* can be replaced by *knows,* it seems here that the underlying grammar of the sentences is quite different. Consider the result of such substitution:

(7) *a* knows the theory of evolution.
(8) *a* knows what his mother tells him.

To be said to know a theory is to be said to know how to describe the theory, to know what it will explain, and so forth. It is thus difficult if not impossible to turn (7) into a *knowing that* construction in many cases. Here we cannot say that *a* knows that thus-and-so describes the theory, and that the theory will explain this-and-that. What it will explain is indeterminate, and so are the number of ways of characterizing it. In practice, knowing a theory exhibits a kind of conventional scientific competence. We get failure of inference from (7) to (2). A scientist may have competence in utilizing a theory without believing that it is the correct theory for explaining some range of phenomena. Indeed, a scientist may learn a theory for the explicit purpose of refuting it. Similar remarks apply to (8). To know what one's mother says is simply to notice what she says and understand it. This is a far cry from believing it true. As in previous cases, it seems presupposed that what she says is partly indeterminate. The indeterminacy of her speech (part of this is the fact that *exactly* what she will say about something is unknown) is reflected by the difficulty of finding a *knowing that* construction that can be regarded as equivalent to (8). We have failure of inference from (8) to (3). The inferences that have failed show that *knowing* does not imply *believing* in the general case. They also indicate that there are *knowing* constructions that may not be reducible in general to *knowing that* constructions.

We will be interested here solely in the analysis of locutions like "*a* knows that *p*" that can be abstracted to a formula like *Kap,* which is intended to exhibit a strong parallel to *Bap.* This abstraction will obviously go hand in hand with a restriction to factual knowledge in some sense that is similar to the sense of factual belief used in the first three chapters. For knowledge, how-ever, some additional analysis of factual content is required.

Let us return to the example of belief in God's exist-ence. A person might claim to know that God exists because God has told him so in a dream. We might want to reject this as a knowledge claim because the manner in which it is supported is not acceptable. This situation introduces the major puzzle connected with knowledge that does not exist for belief. It is sufficient for a person's claim to believe that God exists (provided that the meaning of this claim is sufficiently clear, or is at least mutually agreed on) that he formulate some sentence and believe it to be true. For a knowledge claim, however, the agent is obliged to at least be able to present some sort of evidence for the truth of his claim and to provide some counterargument against any cogent objections to his claim. Knowledge claims are objective or social in some sense, and we expect that they should be capable of being held by a group of ra-tional agents. The temptation is to rule out the dream because it is private information of some kind, or be-cause it utilizes a channel of information (dream con-tent) that is generally unreliable as an indicator of ex-ternal fact. Unless one is an empirical dogmatist, it is not easy to make these objections in a logically coher-ent fashion that preserves all of one's intuitions about what is and isn't knowledge. A lone astronaut return-ing from Mars might have knowledge that is not possible for anyone else to check, and the knowledge would be, in that sense, private. Here it seems easy to suggest that another astronaut could, in principle, verify the observations of the first. But, of course, the first astronaut might have witnessed a unique event in Martian history which no later astronaut could verify.

It seems difficult to deny that the first astronaut knows what he is talking about. Religious initiates could even argue that their claims are superior to those of the astronaut because with a proper course of preparation, anyone could have the same experience of verifying God's existence. In the case of mathematical knowledge, for example, proper training seems to result in common (objective) knowledge not based on obvious empirical information. These observations sketch the enormous difficulty in the way of *defining* a sense of "private" that could distinguish putative religious information from scientific knowledge that can, in principle, be accepted by anyone who studies the evidence. The usual course of procedure is to stipulate that one is interested in an epistemology for science and not worry too much about how an adequate scientific epistemology might differ from an epistemology for other kinds of human activities. This course reflects the assumed pre-eminence of science as an example of rational thought, although that assumption is not without good intuitive backing. To return to the second method of attempting to discriminate against the dream claim, it might be retorted that a channel of information which is generally unreliable may very well prove reliable on certain occasions. The problem is then to find (if possible) some means of distinguishing its reliable from its unreliable performances. In the religious case, it might be argued that God's word would furnish a suitable means for making the discrimination. The purpose here is not at all to poke fun at religious claims to knowledge, or to argue that they stand on all fours with scientific knowledge. Religious claims are here invoked only as representative of knowledge claims that are supposed to rest upon evidence not subject to ordinary scientific analysis. This raises a problem for the boundaries of factual knowledge, since it appears that knowledge claims must be backed by some sort of evidential claims, and it is not at all apparent what sorts of evidential backing should be permitted in an adequate general analysis. The fact is that it is not easy to provide an account of knowledge that fits one's intuitions about paradigm cases of knowledge and non-knowledge claims, no matter how one sees the paradigm cases as lining up.

Empirical dogmatism has attempted to frame a general theory by an appeal to the origins of knowledge. On this view, knowledge must ultimately be reduced to sensory input or to sensory perception, plus whatever can be deductively or inductively deduced from this information. A complete empiricism must either take a view that mathematics and logic are generalizations of experience, or that they represent an arbitrary human convention. Few philosophers now accept empiricism in such a stark form. It seems clear from a mountain of biological evidence that human beings (along with all higher animals) have been genetically structured by the evolutionary process to treat certain stimuli as having a significance that cannot be explained as a deductive or inductive consequence of stimuli properties alone. The best-known case of this is the human ability to learn a language. It seems clear that a child does not mimic the sounds that it hears and then deduce or induce the structure of its native language; rather, the normal human brain has a complex structure that is ready to act on samples of a language so as to create the grammar of the native language of a child utilizing constraints somehow imposed by the brain structure and not by inductive or deductive logic as philosophers have traditionally seen these structures. Once the possibility of innate structure as a component in human knowledge is recognized, empirical dogmatism seems doomed. All that we can do is study human beings to see, in fact, what they know and what part of this knowledge must be attributed to innate structure determined by the evolutionary process. (Of course, it may be the case that even knowledge of the evolutionary process does not, and cannot, offer an explanation of how particular innate structures are developed except in retrospect.) It is then part of science to attempt some explanation of how these postulated innate structures are realized in the human being.

Even without appeal to recent biological considerations, empirical dogmatism seems dubious. Two reasons for this will be examined here. The first supports the arguments of the last paragraph for reliance on some sort of innate structure to explain human knowledge. An agent may say, "I know that I will never set foot in that place again." This decision cannot always be explained merely on the basis of his experiences in the place in question or on his past biography. Another person might well be pleased to have had sufficiently similar experiences. The decision has to be based on what has been called personality and character, and the suggestion is that these are best regarded as internal states realized in an internal and partially innate structure that is simply not a mere product of past experience. The other reason for questioning empirical dogmatism is based on its oversimplified account of sensory input. Traditionally, empiricists have taken the five senses (sight, hearing, touch, taste, and smell) as the ultimate sources of human knowledge, but this suggests a distinction between the inside and the outside of a human body that isn't tenable. One can, for example, know the position of one's leg while lying perfectly still in bed. Here one may not be able to see, hear, smell, or taste the leg in question. The view that knowledge of the position is reducible to touch is dogmatic and false. Knowledge of the position of limbs is partly dependent on internal sensory apparatus sometimes giving rise to what philosophers speak of as sensations, but not always. Empirical dogmatism is not equipped to explain all knowledge based on sensations and certainly not to explain knowledge not based on sensory input—the whole subject depends heavily on neurophysiological research, which seems to be undercutting the results of past philosophical reflection.

The attempt to shed light on the force of the restriction of knowledge to *factual knowledge,* which is designed to include scientific knowledge, mathematical knowledge, and at least some matters of everyday fact, is now seen to founder on the problem of the origins of human knowledge. What is being suggested here is that philosophy is in no position currently to provide a satisfactory account of the origins of knowledge that is useful in attempting to discriminate between what a human being can and cannot know. The reason for this is that any solution to the origins of knowledge is heavily dependent on future results about human biological structure and its significance that only scientific research and development can provide. Philosophy must be content to characterize knowledge independently of its origins. As a result, philosophy cannot say *exactly* what lies within the compass of human knowledge. In this respect, knowledge differs radically from belief. We have seen, by contrast, that nearly any grammatical sentence can be associated with belief. The first important philosophical constraint follows from the observation that knowledge claims do not suffer from the same sort of ambiguity that plagued our analysis of belief claims. Consider once again a variant of DeSousa's example:

> *a* knows that God exists, but *a* knows that *a* doesn't know this.

This seems just false. The corresponding belief assertion (*believes* for *knows* everywhere) can be true because of the ambiguity of *believes* between unconscious and conscious belief. If *knows that* were similarly ambiguous, it might be possible to make this example true by the following interpretation:

> *a* knows (one way—intuition) that God exists, but *a* knows (intuition) that *a* doesn't know (empirically) that God exists.

That this reading is unavailable gives us a reason to suspect that *knows that* is unambiguous. It will here be postulated that *knows that* is unambiguous on the grounds that no knowledge claim can be found that is true because of the fact that, although it is false on one reading, it can be read as true in another way, utilizing an ambiguity in the *knows that* construction.

We cannot conclude from the lack of ambiguity in *knows that* that there is no form of knowledge corresponding to behavioral belief. Indeed, people know many things that they have not consciously formulated about which they can, nonetheless, recognize true claims. But these instances of knowledge, which may correspond to behavioral belief, are marked off grammatically by the *knows how* construction. We may say any of the following:

(9) He knows how to do the backstroke.
(10) She knows how to get good grades.
(11) He knows how to differentiate those equations.

Here we cannot substitute *knows that* for *knows how*. Although the distinctions marked are not always the same, it is not uncommon for languages to have different verbs for kinds of knowledge. As is well known, German marks a distinction by the use of the different verbs *kennen* and *wissen*. We can see from this that knowledge is not related to belief in any easy manner. (In this monograph, we will restrict ourselves to claims apparently true for speakers of English, and not worry about linguistic generalization across various languages.) If a man does something but says nothing, this may give us grounds for saying that he has a (behavioral) belief, but if he does something and says nothing, this may *establish* that he knows how to do something. In such a case, knowledge may be more apparent than belief. This is far from always being the case. A given performance may establish the truth of (9) above, but it may or may not establish the truth of (11), since the candidate may have made a lucky guess in working with the first test equation.

It seems clear that knowing how (in general) is not susceptible to much in the way of philosophical analysis. In particular cases, knowing how may be critically analyzed in terms of the content of the skill in a presumed context. Knowing how may reduce to doing this if thus-and-so, or doing that if this obtains, and so forth. This kind of analysis is substantive when completed—say for the purposes of devising teaching methods for a skill—and it is not at the requisite level of philosophical generality. At the level of philosophical analysis, only trivialities (perhaps a few near trivialities) seem forthcoming. This is one reason why philosophers have generally restricted the analysis of knowledge to *knowing that,* and why we will do so here.

As the reader no doubt suspects, the distinction between knowing how and knowing that is not as clear as the preceding paragraphs have suggested. The grammatical constructions are not always a reliable guide to the distinction that analysis is interested in. Severe difficulties accrue when the fact that saying things is a kind of activity is explicitly taken into account. An agent knows the date of the Battle of Hastings. We can say that he knows that the battle was fought in 1066, or we can say that he knows how to answer a certain question. Where linguistic skill is involved, the two categories often seem to overlap. Again, although *knowing how* often means knowing how to do something, sometimes it means knowing how something else will behave. A scientist who knows how the particle will behave when accelerated may also know that its behavior can be predicted from certain equations and relevant background information. In the face of difficulties with the distinction, and the fact that analysis is to be restricted to *knowing that* for our purposes, we will have to assume that wherever equivalent *knowing how* and *knowing that* analyses are available, analysis of *knowing how* will be considered derivative on the primary analysis of the *knowing that* case. Since it is clear that knowing how to do the backstroke is like many skills in that it cannot be given an equivalent *knowing that* analysis, the restriction to knowing that must be recognized as rather severe, but undertaken in order to bring about the kind of simplification that proved useful in the case of belief.

Any attempt at drawing an analogy between some kind of knowing that and behavioral belief also encounters some difficulty with the fact that we can sometimes say "I know that *p*" where the circumstances are such that *saying* "I know that *p*" seems equivalent to knowing that *p*. Here are three pertinent examples:

(12) I know that the sun is shining.
(13) I know that the Battle of Hastings was fought in 1066.
(14) I know that I'm in pain.

For (12), we imagine a normal human being saying this to a companion while both are standing in blazing sunlight. For (13), we imagine a normal human being saying this to his history teacher who has just asked in exasperation, "Don't you know *anything* about the history of England?" For (14), we imagine a normal human being saying this to his doctor while the doctor is examining the speaker's hand that was caught badly in a lawn mower a short time ago. In all of these circumstances, there seems to be something *odd* about making a knowledge claim. Consider (12). It's possible to construct a scenario besides the suggested circumstance in which merely saying "The sun is shining" makes perfectly good sense. Perhaps the sun hasn't been seen for weeks. Then asserting (12) echoes a surprising but pleasing observation to a friend who has not yet been outdoors. The point is, what does saying "I know that the sun is shining" add to simply saying "The sun is shining"? The suggested answer is: nothing at all in these circumstances. In the suggested circumstances for (12) and (14), the truth of the claims "The sun is shining" and "I'm in pain" is so obvious that the claim to know does not perform the function of revealing that the speaker has no doubts. Can the speaker and the listener doubt that the sun is shining? Can the speaker and the listener doubt that the speaker is in pain? Because of the lack of contrast with possible doubt, the claim to knowledge seems redundant and adds nothing to the simpler claim that can be made in the same circumstances. In considering (13), it should be noted that a claim coupled with dubiety would not be an answer to the question asked. A claim to know something that is quite obviously true in the circumstances is grammatically acceptable, but it should be recognized as a kind of trivial knowledge claim. It is part of the natural history of our schooling that knowledge of various kinds of surface information (dates, places, crucial numbers) is taken as established by the simple ability to produce them on demand. For purposes of analyzing knowledge, it may be best to ignore trivial cases of obviously true knowledge claims. They can be regarded as ruled out by assumption when it seems convenient, or possibly regarded as a limiting case. Exact treatment can be meshed with an adequate analysis of the non-trivial cases.

With a little ingenuity, we can imagine circumstances in which (12), (13), and (14) make non-trivial claims. For (12), we imagine several people in a fallout shelter several months after an atomic explosion. Their knowledge of the outside world is gained by instruments that have been partially damaged in the blast. Here, "I believe that the sun is shining" contrasts with "I know that the sun is shining" as a plausible explanation of the instrument readings may contrast with a full and definitive explanation. We can imagine that the knowledge claim goes along with an understanding of a systematic variation in the readings brought about by the explosion and suddenly recognized by means of a correlation observed in certain data. For (13), we imagine that future archaeologists have been quarreling about the date of the Battle of Hastings due to a newly discovered calendar discrepancy. An archaeologist may discover a definitive means of dating some relic agreed on all hands to be a remnant of the battle. Here, "I believe that the Battle of Hastings was fought in 1066" contrasts with "I know that the Battle of Hastings was fought in 1066" as a plausible account of the date may contrast with the archaeologist's definitive new explanation. (14) is the most difficult example, and some have denied that a scenario can be constructed for it. Perhaps it can be done as follows, although here the contrasting dubiety is provided by a lie on the part of the speaker. General Billingsgate has had his lower left arm shattered by a sniper's bullet. He claims no pain after receiving aid and prepares to direct a major battle. His staff point to obvious behavioral signs of great pain and urge him to retire to the base hospital. Finally he says, "I *know* that I'm in pain, but if I don't direct this battle we don't have a chance."

We will now try to sharpen somewhat the notion of non-trivial knowing that will concern us in the remainder of our investigation. In the case of trivial knowledge, possible doubt will be described as metaphysical. Metaphysical doubt is the sort of corrosive doubt that has been developed by philosophers attempting to promote the viability of some form of skepticism. Doubt whether one is awake or asleep, doubt whether one is under hypnosis or not, doubt whether one might not be the victim of a sufficiently elaborate hoax, doubt whether one is insane, doubt whether memory is accurate—all of these are metaphysical doubts if there is no particular evidence giving rise to the doubt in the particular circumstances. A metaphysical doubt can be worked up, by contrast to evidence in special cases, for any conceivable knowledge claim. Once we have seen how to construct a metaphysical doubt, we can construct a similar doubt to fit the details of any other knowledge claim, or at least for any other knowledge claim similar to the first in certain respects. Let us look back at (12) and (14). To doubt, under the circumstances, that the sun is shining or that one is in pain must be metaphysical. The history example is somewhat different. Everyone knows, so to speak, that the date of the battle is 1066. To doubt on the grounds, say, that all reference books have made the same error is to doubt on metaphysical grounds unless one has positive evidence that the books have all copied a dubious source, or that the date is other than 1066. This sort of metaphysical doubt will not apply to all knowledge, but it can apply to all knowledge of the conventional sort that we noted earlier. Trivial knowledge, knowledge that can be subject only to metaphysical doubt, is probably best regarded in many contexts as not being knowledge at all. Rather, trivial knowledge seems to constitute the brute facts or evidence from which we derive, by various means, many of our positive beliefs and much of our knowledge.

Non-trivial knowledge, by contrast, will always be subject to other than metaphysical doubt. The knower himself will not doubt what he knows, but he will typically be aware of various possible objections to his knowledge claim (reasons why it is doubted by others), and he must know that he can meet all such objections, or at least be able to meet them as they come up, if his knowledge claim is to stick. Brute facts which show some objection false because they are incompatible with the objection are excellent and obvious means for meeting an objection. Other cases will require special treatment and an awareness of context. For example, we may allow that a certain statistical argument can demonstrate the falsity of an objection even though it does not entail the falsity of the objection. With this in mind, we can try to sharpen the notion of non-trivial knowledge in the following way. To say "I know that *p*" is to assert that one can meet all relevant non-metaphysical objections to *p*. In this case, "I believe that I know that *p*" is to assert that one thinks that there is no non-metaphysical objection to *p* that one cannot counter. On our analysis, therefore, "I know that *p*" and "I believe that I know that *p*" have just the relationship that was found earlier between "*p*" and "I believe that *p*" for conscious belief. This is an argument in favor of the analysis. To say "I know that I know that *p*" is to assert that one knows that one can meet all non-metaphysical objections to *p*. In order to assert this, one should have a logically exhaustive catalogue of possible non-metaphysical objections to *p* and know that one can meet them all. Knowing that one knows is being in a very strong position, so strong that it seems unlikely to be found in non-trivial cases of knowledge apart from mathematics, logic, and some fairly straightforward cases of fact. The preceding partial analysis of non-trivial knowledge leaves us in a position where we have to consider knowledge claims piecemeal and with careful regard for context. For each example, we need to consider the range of possible objections to a knowledge claim to see whether they can or cannot be met by the speaker making the knowledge claim. What the analysis achieves is a uniform non-ambiguous reading of "I know that *p*" that is compatible with intuition in at least the cases that we have mentioned so far. The reading of "I know that *p*" gives a perfectly straightforward analysis of the more general "*a* knows that *p*" so that the analysis is at the level which may prove useful for considering general claims about knowledge.

It may be useful, for a moment, to return to the case of God's existence. Our analysis permits a believer to assert "God exists" or "I believe that God exists" without impropriety. The speaker who asserts that God has established His own existence by an appearance in a dream has to face several non-metaphysical objections. Many dream reports have been made in which a God incompatible with the agent reported in the first dream has been said to establish existence. How can a neutral observer accept one report over the other? It is not enough here that the dream should even be regarded as objective in the sense that proper training could cause its reappearance. In the circumstances, no brute fact can stifle the objection, and no other strategy for meeting it seems available. Our previous analysis suggests that the speaker is not entitled to claim knowledge on the basis of the dream report. Solace for the believer is offered in virtue of the fact that it is compatible with this that his dream be true. We compare the astronaut returning from Mars. His memories may be accurate and his beliefs may be true. But it seems reasonable on reflection to deny that he has knowledge unless subsequent investigation turns up facts that controvert all relevant non-metaphysical objections. It's interesting to note that if such facts should be obtained, we might perfectly well say to him, "We admit that you knew all along."

What a man knows, he knows when he is asleep. This does not show the existence of unconscious knowledge any more than a sleeping man shows the existence of unconscious belief. From the analysis given, it seems clear that preparedness to meet objections entails that there is no unconscious knowledge; that is, *knowing that p* such that a person does not realize that he knows that *p*. In objection to this, scenarios such as the following are sometimes put forward:

A: Do you know the decimal expansion of π to four places?

B: No—wait a minute, yes I do! It's 3.1416.

At first *B* doesn't realize or doesn't remember the expansion, and then it occurs to him. Because he so readily recognizes it when it occurs to him, this bears no analogy to unconscious belief. Scenarios like that just suggested typically deal with trivial knowledge claims of the sort verified by producing a statement of the fact said to be known. This situation makes *B*'s remarks entirely sensible.

In this chapter, we have examined the locution *knowing that,* commented on its apparent unambiguous nature, and suggested a partial analysis of the meaning of the locution for the non-trivial sense that forms the focus of philosophical analysis. The trivial sense is not really different. The trivial assertion "I know that *p*" is such that the speaker could meet all non-metaphysical objections. Triviality arises because there aren't any, so the claim is vacuous. We can readily understand it as a limiting case of the partial analysis. This connection preserves the sense in which the locution is unambiguous. We have also seen that there are no proper analogues to behavioral belief or unconscious belief for *knowing that* constructions. In the next chapter, we will explore some relationships between knowing that and conscious and rational belief.

Chapter 5

Knowledge and Belief

In order to facilitate discussion of the relationship between knowing that and conscious or rational belief, we now explicitly introduce a prefix *Ka* which will have similar syntactic properties in formulae abstracting knowledge claims as the prefix *Ba* has for formulae abstracting belief claims. Having introduced such an operator, we can see immediately that the following pair of formulae do not abstract logical truths for any pair of claims, where *p* abstracts some factual sentence:

(1) *Bap* ⊃ *Kap*,
(2) *Kap* ⊃ *Bap*.

That (1) is false for rational human belief is sufficiently obvious given our previous discussion. But we may well raise the question whether (2) should be considered as a postulate in defining a relationship between knowledge and belief for rational agents. According to the partial analysis of knowledge offered in the last chapter, if it is true of a rational agent that he knows that *p*, then he will also believe that *p*, since he can answer any relevant non-metaphysical objection to *p* and therefore has sufficient reason to believe *p*. (2) is then true of a rational agent given what we have said about knowledge and belief to this point. That (2) is true of a rational agent seems to be agreed by most of the philosophers who have proposed any analysis of knowledge.

There is one observation that seems to account for reluctance expressed by some writers to accepting the truth of (2). If what the sentence abstracted to *Kap* says is true, so also is what the sentence abstracted to *Bap* says. But although the sentence abstracted to *Bap*, in these circumstances, says something true, it may be *very misleading* to say the sentence that is so abstracted. The question of what it is appropriate to say must be distinguished from the question of what is true. This distinction is *not* a peculiarity of knowledge or belief claims, but it is important for understanding how we use them. If, as a newspaper reporter, I know that five people have died in a fire and I report that between five and twenty have been killed, what I say is true but misleading. By comparison, there are many occasions on which saying that someone believes something suggests that he merely believes it and doesn't know it. One is usually expected to make the most specific or most relevant claim that he knows or believes to be true. Any weaker claim, even if true, is regarded as misleading because of this expectation. The reporter's claim that five to twenty have died suggests an uncertainty that he knows does not exist. That's why the claim is misleading in the context in which it is made. If *a* knows that *p*, and I know that he does, then when I say "*a* knows that *p*" I am communicating everything, including the fact that he believes that *p*. If, in the same circumstances, I say only "*a* believes that *p*," I am *suggesting* that he doesn't also know that *p*, otherwise I would have said so. My remark is therefore misleading. Although (2) is true, it doesn't follow from (2) that if it is not misleading to say *Kap*, it is also not misleading to say *Bap*. This fact must be kept carefully in mind when using (2) to justify inferences.

The truth of (2) suggests that knowing that *p* is a

special case of believing that *p*. Philosophers have seized on this fact in attempting to analyze knowing that *p*. More formally, they have tried to find conditions for *Kap* in addition to *Bap* that are jointly necessary and sufficient for *Kap*. This would result in an analysis of *Kap* in terms of conscious or rational belief as well as whatever other notions might need to be included in the analysis.

In the previous chapter, a partial analysis of knowledge was offered. This partial analysis was observed to be highly dependent on context, since it does not independently describe a class of relevant non-metaphysical objections, and hence it does not provide an analysis that can readily be applied in particular instances of putative knowledge. The problem is that for any particular knowledge claim, one must examine the circumstances to determine whether there are non-metaphysical objections and whether they can be met in order to determine whether the knowledge claim is true. Any adequate analysis of knowledge should be compatible with our partial analysis, but it would be desirable to find an analysis that is more direct and specific. It has already been determined that the partial analysis is compatible with adopting (2) as a condition on knowledge. The virtue of (2) from the standpoint of analysis is that we may feel that the truth of belief claims can be established in a wide variety of cases. If this start could be complemented with other necessary and sufficient conditions having suitable philosophical properties, it might be possible to find a full analysis of knowledge such that it could be established that its conditions were met in some cases, thus refuting skepticism and enabling assessment of the truth of knowledge claims in a wide variety of cases. These cases would be cases in which all non-metaphysical objections would be met (compatibly with the partial analysis), and the fact that they were met would be established by the available direct evidence which might, so to speak, be sufficient to overwhelm any possible objection.

A widely accepted condition on knowledge, in addition to belief, is that what is known be true. This can be expressed by the following condition:

(3) $Kap \supset p.$

The motivation for this condition is transparent. The following assertion would clearly be contradictory for a rational agent:

(4) $Kap \wedge \sim p.$

If rational agents are excepted, (4) might be true of a well-meaning and sincere agent who claimed to know p and also asserted a sentence equivalent to $\sim p$ simply because the claim was sufficiently complex that he did not recognize the equivalence or the resulting contradiction. The rational agent, however, asserting $\sim p$, cannot consistently assert also that he knows that p. Since $\sim p$ is taken as a fact by the agent, this constitutes an objection to p and to Kap that the agent cannot meet. There is clearly a strong temptation, given this fact, to argue from $\sim p$ to $\sim Kap$, and to make the following a condition on not knowing that p:

(5) $\sim p \supset \sim Kap.$

By Standard Logic, of course, (5) is equivalent to (3), so the acceptance of (5) is equivalent to the acceptance of (3). We will call any attempt to analyze knowledge incorporating (2) and (3) as conditions on Kap a form of the Ideal Analysis (of knowledge).

There is a line of attack on (3) that has not received much attention in the literature. This line of attack can be explored by examining an implicit ambiguity in the partial analysis of knowledge offered in the last chapter. There it was argued that to say "I know that p" is to assert that one can meet all relevant non-metaphysical objections to p. Two more specific readings of the last clause are possible as follows:

(6) One can meet all current relevant non-metaphysical objections to p.

(7) One can meet all possible relevant non-metaphysical objections to p.

Which of these readings is taken as correct has important consequences for the resulting analysis of knowledge.

We first examine the conception of knowledge that is obtained if (7) is taken as the preferred reading. It seems pretty clear that this reading gives us a version of the Ideal Analysis. Should one be able to meet all possible relevant non-metaphysical objections to p, it would seem to follow that p is true. For if p were not true, then there would be a cogent possible objection to p that could not be met. A sentence that can be substituted for p cannot have a changing truth value on the normal analysis. Therefore, once a person knows that p because he has sufficient evidence to rule out all possible relevant non-metaphysical objections, we expect that Kap should remain true. Since we want to say this, we need to stipulate that meeting an objection must be as strong a notion as demonstrating its falsehood and not merely replying to it in some fashion. This would guarantee refuting the objection in all possible circumstances. Given such a reading, (7) provides us with a version of the partial analysis that is compatible with any adequate version of the Ideal Analysis.

Reading (6) seems not to be compatible with the

Ideal Analysis. On reading (6), to know that p is merely to be able to meet all *current* relevant non-metaphysical objections to p. The plain suggestion is that it is quite possible for scientific advances to expose new objections to p that were previously not thought of. Suppose we think of asserting p as having this significance: There are no possible relevant non-metaphysical objections to p that can't be met. Then our reading of (3) is something like this:

(8) If a can meet all current relevant non-metaphysical objections to p, then there are no possible relevant non-metaphysical objections to p that can't be met.

For arbitrary agents, even rational agents, (8) is clearly false. On reading (6), therefore, we don't have a version of the Ideal Analysis. Let us call any analysis of knowledge compatible with reading (6) a form of the Pragmatic Analysis (of knowledge).

There are several points to notice about the Pragmatic Analysis. Suppose *Kap* can be asserted. It is compatible with this that $\sim p$ is true. Now suppose that some new relevant non-metaphysical objection to p is discovered which can't be met. (In a sense, this raises the possibility that, compatibly with current knowledge, $\sim p$ might be true.) *Kap* is no longer true. Should $\sim p$ now be discovered true, then *Kap* is certainly not true. We have the same situation that we had on the Ideal Analysis, $\sim p$ and *Kap* cannot be jointly asserted by a rational agent. The difference in the situation is provided by involvement with temporality. On both analyses, once $\sim p$ is found to be true, one must conclude that a rational agent can't know that p. The difference comes in connection with our attitude towards past knowledge claims. On the Ideal Analysis, if $\sim p$ is true, one could never have known that *p*. On the Pragmatic Analysis, the situation is somewhat different. Consider the following pair of assertions:

(9) I used to know that if I pressed button A, the temperature would reach safe levels within ten minutes.

(10) Kit Carson knew that since the edges of the tracks were sharp, the Indians could be overtaken within two hours.

These assertions point to contexts in which relevant objections show a development over time. It doesn't follow logically or from the laws of nature that the Indians can be caught given the shape of their tracks. The Indians were perhaps heading for a rendezvous with a helicopter. They couldn't have (non-metaphysically) in Kit Carson's time, so Kit Carson did know something, but a modern Kit Carson would have to allow for helicopters. Again, the scientist of (9) may be reacting to a change in the design of his apparatus, or to its unexpected performance in a new application. These examples indicate that the Pragmatic Analysis is compatible with some facts about the way in which we ordinarily conceive of knowledge that the Ideal Analysis cannot explain.

The divergence between Ideal Analysis and Pragmatic Analysis is related to a situation which is not uncommon in analytic philosophy. A philosopher of science may define a notion of scientific explanation based on a conception of a scientific law as a generalization to which *there are no counterexamples* (now or ever). No one may be able to show such an *analysis* defective by counterexample, but it has the consequence that one can never tell whether some generalization *is* a scientific law because one can never rule out the later appearance of a counterexample provided that the generalization has empirical content. Because of this, one can never tell whether a putative explanation involving a generalization is actually an explanation. Such idealization is common in philosophy, and the strategy of analysis suggests that the analyzed notions be regarded as ideal types that actual instances of scientific practice can only approximate. We had an example of such idealization earlier in the concept of a rational belief structure. In this case, however, we had a firm bridge from ordinary concepts to the ideal concept through such notions as consistency. Although an actual agent cannot have an infinite number of beliefs, we call him rational if he adjusts his beliefs on discovery of an inconsistency. He is warranted in asserting that his beliefs are consistent if at the time of assertion he has not been able (after a reasonable attempt) to find a counterexample. In the scientific case, a proposed explanation is warranted if a reasonable attempt to refute the laws utilized has not turned up a counterexample to them. When a counterexample appears, the explanation must be abandoned. *Fallibilism* is sometimes used to refer to the position that counterexamples will almost certainly turn up in the future to any current generalization. Fallibilism plus the ideal conception of scientific law suggests that we can produce no actual examples of a scientific explanation. For any actual example, we can easily construct an imagined circumstance in which it would fail. This has led many philosophers to propose that an analysis of explanation should be provided that is actually instanced in scientific practice. Anytime these philosophers produce an analysis, it will be subject to counterexample in an idealized but logically possible situation. The argument about the appropriate level for philosophical analysis of scientific explanation cannot be resolved here, but an appreciation of its existence is important. A similar point divides Pragmatic Analysis from Ideal Analysis. On both analyses, an actual agent will revise his claims in the light of certain kinds of information. The Pragmatic Analysis, however, can seemingly be realized in actual practice while the Ideal Analysis cannot. In given circumstances, a man may know that he can handle any relevant current non-metaphysical objection, but he can never know that he can handle any possible objection unless he places undue reliance on some current conception of the scope of logical possibility. Fallibilism plus the Ideal Analysis entails that we cannot be sure that we know anything (at some given time). Fallibilism plus the Pragmatic Analysis allows us to be sure that we know in at least some cases (at some given time). If the analysis of knowledge is to provide the result that knowledge claims are special instances of belief claims, some decision about what kind of belief claims are involved needs to be made. Since we have seen that various belief structures can either be realized in human agents, or can be taken as idealizations of actual belief structures, it would apparently be fruitful to have a conception of knowledge permitting knowledge to be instantiated in some actual cases. This line of reasoning provides some motivation for attempting a Pragmatic Analysis, but the fact is that attempts to develop an Ideal Analysis have dominated the literature. One reason for this is that (2) and (3) have natural readings in Standard Logic for which there is considerable intuitive defense, as we have seen. The hope is that one can then use the powerful resources of Standard Logic to develop consequences of conditions (2) and (3) along with whatever else is required. For the time being, therefore, we will examine the development of Ideal Analysis.

True belief, which is what conditions (2) and (3) amount to, is clearly not *equivalent* to knowledge. The intuition here is that a man who has true belief may be just lucky, and consequently his claim to knowledge does not have the support that it should have. This is supported by the partial analysis if he cannot meet objections, as we can well imagine in an actual case. Ideal Analysis has usually attempted to provide another condition on true belief that would insure that some subclass of a person's true beliefs was equivalent to the class of things that he could be said to know. The desired condition is intuitively referred to as justification or complete justification. If justification or complete justification can be properly spelled out, this version of the Ideal Analysis seems quite promising. How is this approach related to the partial analysis previously offered? Our partial analysis suggests that a person can be said to know when he can eliminate relevant non-metaphysical objections. The current version of Ideal Analysis suggests that a person can be said to know when he has overwhelming evidence for what he claims to know. Actually, while overwhelming evidence could rule out all objections to a claim, we can imagine that it does not, so the two lines of analysis may appear to be distinct. This apparent distinction can be circumvented when we remember that it is knowledge that is under discussion. A useful analogy can be drawn between some concepts required here and a pair of concepts that we used in talking about rational belief. Justified true belief analyses depend on something like the likelihood assumption and suggest that a belief with sufficient likelihood that is also true is equivalent to a knowledge claim. Our partial analysis apparently ignores likelihood and refers to establishing some claim against rival claims. This strategy bears many resemblances to the third strategy for obtaining relief from the lottery paradox offered in Chapter 3. Since we were discussing *justified* belief in Chapter 3 in connection with the likelihood assumption for rationality, it is not surprising that some connections exist between that discussion and our current discussion. The differences between the strategies for consistent rational belief disappear when they are reinterpreted in connection with knowledge claims. In the case of knowledge, we are trying to establish the truth of a sentence and rule out the truth of all alternative sentences. This can't be done on the evidence unless the likelihood becomes arbitrarily high, so the strategies become equivalent if we are considering a range of rival knowledge claims such that there is evidence favoring only one claim of any pair of claims in which we are interested. Ideal Analysis and our partial analysis mesh satisfactorily if we consider claims against a background of rival claims and utilize a notion of justification strong enough to rule out any counterexamples in which a non-metaphysical objection favoring one of the rival claims is developed.

The discussion of likelihood in Chapter 3 was in connection with beliefs that might be false. It was not necessary there to point out that a false sentence might, in certain circumstances, have as high a likelihood as one might care to stipulate. Suppose we are, in fact, randomly tossing a fair coin, but we do not know whether the coin we are tossing is fair, or is a coin resembling the fair coin; that is, a coin heavily biased towards heads that was constructed in our laboratory for demonstration purposes. The fair coin could (if we were unlucky) show nothing but heads for any number of actual tosses, raising the likelihood that we were, in fact, tossing the biased coin rather than the fair coin to any stipulated value. This is sufficient to show that likelihood cannot establish truth in the general case. (The third strategy for avoiding the lottery paradox doesn't deny this—it counsels us to bet that we won't be unlucky very often.) Now the Ideal Analysis for justified belief stipulates what is justifiably believed be true, so perhaps this can rule out the awkward case where what is believed on high likelihood is false.

Let us look at the Ideal Analysis in a more formal mode. According to the analysis, a knows that p if and only if the following conditions are satisfied:

(11) *Bap.*
(12) *p.*
(13) a is justified (or completely justified) in believing p.

The details of the relationship of justification or complete justification will not concern us. It suffices to say that this relationship makes implicit reference to evidence that provides the justification, and the relationship should not be so strong that evidence that satisfies it always implies p. Justification need not be discussed in greater detail here because of a style of counterexample (due to Edmund L. Gettier) that seems to be decisive against any analysis utilizing (11), (12), and (13) or roughly equivalent conditions. Let a's evidence be a set of sentences E (stipulated to consist solely of true sentences) that justifies or completely justifies a hypothesis h. We now stipulate that although h is false, it has a logical consequence p, which is true. It will be assumed for the moment that if E justifies or completely justifies h, and p is a consequence of h, that E also completely justifies p. Suppose that a believes p because of the evidence E. Then conditions (11)–

(13) are satisfied for this particular example by stipulation. The circumstances may be such, however, that *a* would not be said to know that *p*.

To see how the structure of a simple Gettier counterexample can be realized in a particular case, we will look at one of Gettier's examples. Let *a* have as much evidence as the analysis of justification requires for the truth of the following claim:

(14) Jones owns a Ford.

We can imagine that *a* has seen Jones driving one for years, that Jones is a close friend and a coworker, and that *a* has seen Jones's registration, and so forth. (14) implies both of the following:

(15) Jones owns a Ford, or Brown is in Boston.
(16) Jones owns a Ford, or Brown is in New York.

Now suppose that Jones does not own a Ford in spite of the evidence (he just traded it on impulse for a Chevrolet) and that Brown, as a matter of fact, is in Boston even though *a* has no idea where Brown is. Since (15) and (16) are logical consequences of (14), and *a* is presumed rational, we can suppose that *a* believes (15) and (16). Now, if (15) is taken as *p* for the conditions of the last paragraph, conditions (11)–(13) hold for (15) given the details of the situation. We would not want to say that *a* knows that (15), however, since it is just a lucky coincidence that (15) is true.

Gettier counterexamples have stimulated an enormous literature devoted to the problem of a more successful analysis of knowledge. The motivation for this may be that if Gettier counterexamples succeed, the development of some form of Ideal Analysis seems virtually ruled out—and most philosophers have felt that

Ideal Analysis offers the correct general approach to an analysis of knowledge. Subsequent discussion has generally accepted the intuition that *a* does not know that *p* in a Gettier counterexample, and various ways of adding one or more new conditions to (11)–(13) have been proposed so as to find conditions that are both necessary and sufficient for knowledge. In other words, writers have asked the question why the agent in a Gettier counterexample does not know. Then they have attempted to turn their answer to that question into a condition that would insure knowledge in other cases.

One strategy is to point out that if (14) comes to be known to be false, (15) and (16) saddle *a* with the incompatible beliefs that Brown is in Boston and that he is in New York. (We assume *a* is sufficiently familiar with geography to remember that Brown can't be in both places, but logic requires that this be stipulated.) Therefore *a* should not hold (15) and (16) among his beliefs. If he just holds (15), since he cannot justify "Brown is in Boston" his belief in (15) as a knowledge claim cannot survive the discovery that (14) is false. To meet this objection and others that are tied rather closely to features of the original example, we can introduce a slightly different example (also proposed by Gettier). We have seen that *a* and Jones work in the same office. Let *a* believe the following claim instead of either (15) or (16):

(17) Someone in my office owns a Ford.

(17) follows from (14) and the fact about Jones's place of employment. (17) remains true when (14) is discovered false provided only that someone else in the office owns a Ford, someone that *a* may very well not know owns a Ford. Here we can say that Jones does

not know (17) even though discovering the falsity of (14) does not entail that he has contradictory beliefs. The intuition exploited in this paragraph does explain why the Gettier counterexamples are counterexamples in certain selected cases, but it seems clear that correcting merely this defect cannot lead to a new condition in addition to (11)–(13) that yields a satisfactory total analysis. In particular, it fails to explain why *a* doesn't know (17) in the revised counterexample.

A related observation about the Gettier counterexamples is that they rely on the principle that if a person is completely justified in believing *s*, then he is completely justified in believing any logical consequence of *s*. One can hold that this principle is not true in general, although both attack and defense of the principle depend upon clarifying what is meant by complete justification. Whatever complete justification is, it is usually said to be compatible with our being completely justified in believing something that is false. Earlier, in connection with rational belief, we saw that the assumptions of detachment, deductivity, and likelihood generated a paradox, and that at least one of them required relaxation. If complete justification is a version of a likelihood notion, then the principle cited about complete justification may entail a paradox, since it utilizes the notion of logical consequence and detachment of belief. We would get a paradox, for example, if we adopted the following principle: If *a* is completely justified in believing *p*, and *a* is completely justified in believing *q*, then *a* is completely justified in believing $(p \land q)$. Suppose we already have beliefs, in particular a belief *s* and a logical consequence of *s* which we will refer to as *t*, and then we acquire new evidence. What is true is the following: The likelihood of a belief *s* on the total evidence (old and new) is such that whatever it is, t will have a likelihood at least as great. But in this situation, we need to compare these likelihoods with the strength of the beliefs in s and t that we started with before the new evidence was obtained. What can happen is that where there is a much higher previous strength of belief in t than in s, the likelihood of s and t taking the new evidence into account is the same for both and is assigned a number higher than that assigned to the old strength of belief in s and lower than the old strength of belief in t. Since s entails t, here is a situation where we may be completely justified in believing s and in believing t even though we are less sure of t than we were beforehand. The possibility that we might be completely justified in believing something that we are less sure of than before raises a difficulty for the clarification of the notion of complete justification. Since the new evidence has lowered our strength of belief in t, it is not easy to see intuitively how we could have been completely justified in believing it beforehand. It might also be noted that in terms of our intuitions about these matters, there are some situations that seem to deny outright the principle about complete justification previously cited. A scientist might be (intuitively) completely justified in accepting a new theory in some formulation even though it entails some consequences that are, to put it mildly, completely incredible. Indeed, while accepting the theory, he may suspend belief in these consequences until relevant experimental data is available. This is a difficult case since the scientist is likely to consider belief in a revised version of the theory (should later data force revision) as belief in the same theory, but we are interested primarily in his attitude *before* the data is available. There are, then, some interesting grounds for questioning whether the cited principle should be regarded as an axiom for a formalized concept of complete justification. At the same time, these objections do not touch the examples we have considered, so that reason to doubt the general case does not suggest in itself a useful new condition for amending the analysis. In a setting as bare as that provided by the examples, if *a* is completely justified in his intermediate beliefs, it seems that he is also completely justified in the beliefs that he infers from these. It is therefore doubtful that one could find an analysis of complete justification that provided a satisfactory analysis of knowledge and yet would explain the failure of knowledge to obtain in the simple Gettier counterexamples provided that *a* can have as much evidence as is possible compatibly with some false belief.

The position in which we find ourselves in connection with the observation that if *a* is completely justified in believing *s*, then he is completely justified in believing any logical consequence of *s*, is that while it may not be true in general, it can't always be false either. This suggests another strategy. If we assume that there are cases of human knowledge and that people can obtain knowledge by reasoning, we run into the difficulty that the agent's steps of reasoning in a simple Gettier counterexample are instances of a pattern of inductive inference (that seems justified if any such inference is) coupled with a deductive inference. We might claim that although this pattern of two-step inference does not yield knowledge, some other patterns of inference (perhaps utilizing a third sort of inference step) might produce knowledge. Then we could argue that if an agent reasons according to one of these acceptable patterns, he has knowledge, even though he might have reasoned according to an unacceptable pattern. Gilbert Harman has made such a proposal utilizing a notion of "inference to the best explanation." "Inference to the best explanation" is inference from evidence to that hypothesis which would best *explain* it. Such a hypothesis need not have the highest likelihood of any hypothesis on the evidence. The inductive inference of the Gettier counterexamples is not an "inference to the best explanation" in Harman's sense, and the pattern of reasoning is therefore defective from the point of view of producing knowledge. What this strategy suggests is that one has knowledge if one reasons in a way that an ideally rational agent would reason utilizing one of the preferred patterns, or if one reasons in such a fashion that such rational reasoning is, in some sense, embedded in one's reasoning. One might also place such restrictions on the reasoning as that the reasoning not pass through any false sentences in realizing a preferred structure. The suggestion is interesting, but it is far from being worked out in any adequate detail. It requires a sense of inference or correct reasoning pattern that is not reducible to inductive and deductive steps in the classic sense, and it is much easier to suggest the existence of such patterns than to work them out in such a fashion that designated patterns always lead to knowledge when correctly instantiated. "Inference to the best explanation," for example, remains an intuitive notion that can be illustrated in certain contexts, but for which no general canons of inference are available.

The third observation about the Gettier counterexamples to be made here is a consequence of the partial analysis of the last chapter. Consider the example where a is completely justified in believing (14), and this leads him to believe (17) which is true. (14) is in fact false, so there must be evidence that could be added to E that would result in a's not being completely justified in believing (14). The abstract structure of the example is that *a* is completely justified by evidence *E* in believing some (false) sentence *f* from which he infers *p* and on the basis of which he believes *p*. We can't say that this should not be permitted because there is a sentence that could be added to *E* that would establish the falsity of *f*, since ~*f* is always available to play this role. Similarly, we cannot rule this out because there is a true sentence that can be added to *E* that establishes the falsity of *f*, for this condition would preclude ever having complete justification for a false sentence. The notion of *total available evidence* might be tried, except that this is open to counterexample if the total available evidence happens to be misleading. What about total available evidence which *a* is completely justified in believing true or false? In our example, *a* may be completely justified in believing ~(14) false, although it is in fact true. Perhaps a situation where a rational agent *a* believes, and is completely justified in believing, a true sentence false that would (if considered true) result in his not being completely justified in believing *p* is a situation open to a Gettier counterexample. Where this is not the case and justified true belief obtains, perhaps we can find knowledge. This suggestion results in an *ad hoc* definition with the following property: If *a* knows that *p* according to the definition, because *a* is not completely justified in believing ~*f* false, others can know that ~*p* because they *are* completely justified in believing ~*f* false. If we place *a* and all others on an equal footing, we are back in circumstances where the evidence may be misleading, and a Gettier counterexample is available. The third observation doesn't seem to lead to any potentially viable proposal for repairing the Ideal Analysis.

The fourth observation about the Gettier counterexamples is that agent *a* is involved, in some sense, with a false sentence. Let us look at an abstract formulation of the logic of the counterexamples again. An agent has evidence (suppose it true) that is summarized in a sentence E, E completely justifies f (which is false), f entails p (which is true), and hence a believes that p and is completely justified in so doing. One objection to this is that a may not believe that p *because* he believes that f, even though he is completely justified in so doing. So we assume, in addition, that a believes that p because he believes f (whether consciously or unconsciously), and because he takes E as his evidence for f, and because these facts in conjunction with his recognition of the entailment between f and p led him to believe that p. We have assumed something like this earlier where it seemed important. Now perhaps we want to say that a does not know that p under the circumstances because the route he takes from believing E to believing that p passes through a false sentence. We have to be wary of saying that a knows that p if and only if (11)–(13) are satisfied and a's route from E to p involves no false assertion. For example, a may think of E, and then believe that p, without *consciously* thinking about f at all. In this case, a's route may include unconscious or suppressed steps, so we need to make some conjectures about how a rational agent would actually reason. Let us suppose that a full explanation of the process of human reasoning tells us that a rational agent a will only pass from believing that E to believing that p (in the circumstances) by formulating f and inferring p, whether this is done consciously or not. It is because we must posit a psychology, of which we spoke mysteriously in the first sentence of this paragraph, about a being involved *in some sense* with a false sentence. This point of view leads to the suggestion that a knows that p if and only if he (in fact) can pass from believing E to believing that p through a route that utilizes only true intermediate steps that are not accidentally true in some sense to be specified, and in fact does pass from E to p through such a route.

We have met this idea earlier in the suggestion that some form of inference other than deductive or inductive inference in the traditional sense might be involved. Then we can require that the patterns utilizing this new form not involve false propositions. Many philosophers have doubted that such a form of inference exists. Since we have mentioned the other possibility, we will restrict ourselves here to views utilizing only deductive and inductive inference.

The strategy that develops the idea that knowledge should be obtained by a route utilizing only true intermediate steps must specify a sense in which these steps are not accidentally true. Clearly, specifying merely that the intermediate steps be true is unsatisfactory. On the one hand, they might all be true even though knowledge fails. Consider agent a and (14) again. Suppose a's evidence true, that it completely justifies him in believing (14), and that (14) is also true. But Jones has had a busy day. He no sooner sold his old Ford and bought a Chevrolet in the morning than he was informed that he had won a Ford in a raffle. Although (14) is true, it is not because Jones owns the Ford a thinks that he does. Under these circumstances, a does not seem to know that Jones owns a Ford. Jones owns a Ford only as the result of a lucky accident, and not as the man who explains the evidence which a prizes. If a discovers the morning sale before hearing of the raffle, he would have to retract his knowledge claim. Now suppose that a is a scientist and knows that p because of 1000 experiments and their results, all of which he thinks are summarized by some experimental generalization. The generalization is true, but experiment #469 is not an instance of it due to a copying error by one of his assistants. But *a* can meet this objection by *throwing out* this evidence and still know that *p*. Indeed, if *a* has a means of passing from *E* to *p* through a chain of true sentences sufficient to yield knowledge of *p*, he need not be embarrassed by other lines he has explored (possibly conflated with the sufficient line) that are not sufficient to yield knowledge because they contain irrelevant information. He can simply ignore them as proven wrong by the sufficient line or as entirely irrelevant. Mere truth in intermediate steps seems actually neither necessary nor sufficient.

Most of the recent manifestations of the strategy we are exploring have avoided complete skepticism in the face of the Gettier counterexamples by the following strategy. Knowledge is regarded as basic or non-basic. Basic knowledge is defined as knowledge not obtained by inference; that is, knowledge that is in some sense *directly evident*. Basic knowledge and all logical consequences of basic knowledge are not subject to Gettier counterexamples. This preliminary move is apparently designed to show (among other things) that the Gettier counterexamples do not completely devastate *any* analysis of knowledge, although it accomplishes this move by postulation unless the existence of basic knowledge can be independently established, perhaps by illustrative example. We are primarily interested in knowledge obtained from basic knowledge closed under logical consequence (as well as other kinds of true evidence, if the conditions on basic knowledge permit this). The knowledge is then to be obtained by some sort of inductive inference given our current restrictions. Unless there is such knowledge, the existence of scientific knowledge, for example, seems threatened by our inability to find an Ideal Analysis that can define its abstract features.

We then need some variation in the following theme. Suppose our agent has a batch of basic knowledge or evidence of some kind that is not based inferentially on further evidence. We call this batch of information *b*. Suppose that *b*, in conjunction with deductive Standard Logic and some kind of inductive logic explicating a notion of justification, only permits an agent to detach true beliefs, and in particular does not justify him in believing *anything* false. Then we might hold that true beliefs obtained from *b* constitute knowledge. The intuitive idea seems interesting, but there are a number of pitfalls in working it out in any detail.

Now we can look back at the example about *a* and his false belief (14) that Jones owns a Ford, and his true belief (17) that someone owns a Ford. The belief *a* has in (14) is based on a conjunction of evidential sentences that look like the following:

(18) Jones has been seen with an auto registration for a Ford, and Jones is always seen driving a Ford, and so on.

Let us abstract (18) for our purposes to the following:

(19) $A_j \wedge B_j \wedge C_j \wedge \ldots \wedge N_j$.

A_j abstracts the claim that Jones has an automobile registration for a Ford, and so forth. Concept (19) confers evidence on (14) which is false, and (14) in turn entails (17) which is true but which is not known by *a*.

Perhaps we could try something like the following. *Kap* is true if and only if (i) *p*, (ii) *Bap*, and (iii) *a* has evidence for *p* which completely justifies only what is true. There are easy counterexamples to this.

One (due to Gettier) points out that the disjunction of (19) and (17) is a true sentence that is evidence for (17) and justifies it completely since one disjunct does so by hypothesis and the other entails it. This disjunction doesn't appear to justify any false sentence. Another counterexample (due to Fred Feldman) points out that (19) entails the following:

(20) $(\exists x)(Ax \wedge Bx \wedge Cx \wedge \ldots \wedge Nx)$.

(20) is evidence for (17) and doesn't appear to justify any false sentence.

In both counterexamples to the suggestion that we use the condition that a has evidence for p which completely justifies only what is true, evidential sentences were used which had this property, but which, in turn, were based on whatever evidence a has for (19). Since (19) completely justifies (14) which is false, and this evidence justifies (19) if complete justification is transitive (at least in these circumstances), a's basic knowledge or ultimate evidence does not seem to permit a to know anything inferentially. There is one aspect of this situation that can nonetheless still be exploited. Although the total evidence completely justifies (19), each bit of evidence presumably justifies only (or justifies with the right selection of other bits) one of the conjuncts of (19). So we have this situation. (19) is equivalent to a *conjunction* of sentences *each* of which is justified by some of the evidence in a's ultimate evidence. If the ultimate evidence can be arranged into pieces (sentences incorporating the right selection of bits) that justify no false sentences and none of which justify (19) as a whole, we can say that (19) is justified by a set of sentences none of which justifies a false sentence, but (17) does not have this property because it is justified by (19) which does justify the false (14).

In these circumstances, we can regard the evidence as playing the role of the hypothetical batch of basic knowledge *b* described earlier. The problem, of course, is to work out a general characterization of an arrangement of evidence that has just the desired properties, and so far no one has been able to do this.

Our first attempt at constructing an adequate Ideal Analysis based on the fourth observation about the Gettier counterexamples is based on a notion of non-accidentally true inferential steps whose truth is guaranteed by an evidential base with certain desirable properties. Another attempt can be made to rule out accidental truth by utilizing the notion of causation.

A causal analysis of knowledge based on non-accidentally true intermediate steps requires that a causal chain connect *p* and *Bap* in some fashion. For this purpose, certain kinds of inferences can be regarded as part of a causal chain. A case that would be included in any such analysis would be the case where an event *p* is connected to certain evidential events *q* by a causal chain, *a* sees *q* (his evidence), consequently believes that *q* occurred, and hence believes that *p*. In particular, it should be noted that a causal account of perception is involved in the move from *q* to *Baq*. This analysis attacks the counterexamples at the point of the possible causal chain from *p* to *q*. In Gettier counterexamples, the evidence is *not* linked appropriately to what the person believes (correctly) is the case. The fact of ownership which makes (17) true does not cause the evidence that Jones takes to completely justify that fact. Other causal patterns than the simple evidential pattern cited would be required for any full analysis, but it seems clear that utilizing causal chains and inferential chains in various patterns cannot supply the missing condition. To begin with, there are severe difficulties in the analysis of causal chains which infest the use of these chains in any total causal theory of perception. For example, *a* is expecting his sweetheart on the next packet boat. He looks across the water and suddenly exclaims (on the basis of a small speck he thinks he sees on the horizon), "Here comes the packet boat!" The speck is the packet boat, and *a* is correct, so a causal chain exists. But *a* did not know that the speck was the boat since the speck might have been that of some other (completely unexpected) boat due to a lack of visual detail. There is no doubt that causal chains are involved in perception. But because of the phenomenon of (internal) mental state (expectation, for example) and the possible existence of indeterministic mechanisms as well as causal mechanisms involved in perception, simply invoking causal chains does not seem to offer a total account of knowledge although it may provide sufficient conditions for knowledge in certain circumstances. In many cases, one causal chain may mask another in a way that our rational agent cannot discern. Agent *a* happens on a decapitated body which he recognizes as that of his friend Brown. (This example is due to Brian Skyrms.) Under the circumstances, *a* knows that Brown is dead, but it happens that there is no causal chain connecting death and decapitation. Brown was killed by a blow to the head and decapitation accidentally occurred later on as the body was being moved. True, decapitation might not have occurred if the blow to the head had not been struck, but in this sense, many events might be casually related in a way that would prove awkward for a causal theory. It seems, then, that the causal Ideal Analysis will only prove illuminating in special cases.

This brings us to the end of a rather discouraging survey of attempts to work out a satisfactory Ideal

Analysis. The available attempts are defective or inadequate, and the prospects for completing an Ideal Analysis do not seem bright. Among the possibilities, the two most viable proposals seem to involve either working out a set of rational inferences that, when they do not as a matter of fact involve a false sentence in any inferential step, yield knowledge, or working out a notion of complete justification which, when it applies to evidence that does not as a matter of fact justify any false sentence, yields knowledge. Both analyses, even when complete, would be difficult to instantiate in practice. The reason for this is the requirement that all sentences potentially related to the evidence and the claim that is said to be known must as a matter of fact be known to be true if we are to know that we have a case of knowledge. But any *particular* knowledge claim involving any non-deductive inferential step could always be supposed to involve some false sentence by a sort of Gettier perspective. Since we allow that justification *might* be justification of a false sentence, or that preferred inference might pass through a false sentence, we can simply imagine the circumstances to be just those in which one of these things occurs. Then the agent doesn't know.

We start with the intuition that skepticism is wrong and that we have knowledge. Further, we assume that we have some knowledge which is inferential, that is, does not constitute trivial or basic knowledge and deductive consequences of the same. But if we look at any particular case, we can imagine that it will fail due to bad luck on the part of the knower realized in a logically possible situation in which his evidence is misleading in some way. We have a situation here which is reminiscent of the lottery paradox. In the lottery paradox (before resolution by one of the strategies) we found it plausible to scrutinize each ticket and conclude that it would not win, even though this jarred with the fact that we knew that one of the tickets had to win. Let us examine a wide group of knowledge claims. Some of these claims will have better evidence, or better structure, than the others. To facilitate comparison with the lottery paradox, we will examine only those claims meeting our highest standards on some version of the Ideal Analysis. We may well feel that within this class of knowledge claims there must be some that aren't the victims of bad luck, even though as we examine the claims one by one we can imagine for each claim that there are circumstances in which it is involved with a false sentence that renders it void. One by one, we reject the claims, even though this jars with our feeling that it is foolish to suppose that they are all rendered void by these hypothetical circumstances. Skepticism points to the one possibility that they *are* all void, but this entails that everyone is faced with misleading evidence for what he claims to know, and we can arrange circumstances in which this is revealed as the blatantly absurd metaphysical ploy we know it to be.

The difficulties we have encountered in attempting to develop a version of the Ideal Analysis can be compared to the difficulties that have been traditionally encountered in attempting to frame a notion of valid inductive inference. A simple form of the problem can easily be stated. (This should be regarded as a reminder for our present purposes and not as an exposition of inductive inferential patterns in general.) Suppose all observed A's have been B's, and there remain some unobserved A's. Under what circumstances is it legitimate to infer that all the A's ever to be observed will also be B's? In more general problems, we may be interested in drawing an inference from a statistic true of a limited sample of a population to a related statistic of the whole population. It is easy to show that no rules of inference or conditions set on the sample or the properties involved can insure the truth of inductively inferred claims. In each case of a genuine inductive inference based on some rule, we can cite logically possible cases in which the sample is misleading or biased, and the rule licenses an inference to a false conclusion. One position compatible with the evidence is inductive skepticism. The advocate charges that there is no knowledge of the future and relentlessly develops counterexamples to proposed rules of inference. This position, while consistent with the evidence, is surely unable to draw distinctions that we can recognize in practice between good experimental design and poor experimental design. The practicing scientist of a philosophical or methodologically inclined bent may well recognize the force of skepticism, and he may see that his rules of inference are sound for only certain kinds of properties or statistics, and for samples that are not biased. Indeed, stated so as to be sound, the rules of inference, *given a random as opposed to a biased sample,* are deductive trivialities. In practice, then, the scientist does what he can to see that his samples aren't biased although he cannot know that they are not biased at the time he makes an inductive inference. He tries to control sources of bias that have been observed retrospectively in past experiments, and he should stand ready to revise design if some relevant non-metaphysical reason for suspecting bias should be produced against his design. For each individual inference, the scientist or the philosopher cannot show that it isn't completely wide of the mark, but it can be argued that the overall strategy employed in all inferences is as systematic and defensible as any. And then there is, of course, the past record of achievement of sophisticated experimental design.

In the case of inductive inference, it is not necessary that any particular inference be singled out as most likely to succeed. The chance of attaining some group objective of science is supposed to be maximized by the successes within a group of inferences which cannot be adjudicated in advance. The situation with knowledge is not exactly parallel. Here we are not satisfied to feel that a certain percentage of knowledge claims are satisfactory, because we feel that certain specific knowledge claims *must* constitute knowledge or the concept is not of any use to us. The Gettier counterexamples then point to the suggestion that if any particular knowledge claim can be unlucky, perhaps the whole notion of knowledge by inference is dispensible in a more sophisticated environment, say in science, and inferred, justified true belief (which is not knowledge on the Ideal Analysis) is the best we can hope for. Knowledge would then be comparable to valid rules of inference which could insure truth, a concept that is but the interesting legacy of a dark philosophical past. These and other issues will be explored from the perspective of the Pragmatic Analysis in the next chapter.

Chapter 6

Pragmatic Analysis

To this point, we have not considered iterated knowledge operators as we did iterated belief operators earlier. Consider the following formulae, where p abstracts some factual sentence:

(1) $KaKap \supset Kap$.
(2) $Kap \supset KaKap$.

Clearly (1) seems to be true, but (2) is the subject of considerable controversy. It may be useful to begin a discussion by indicating the connection between Ideal Analysis and an acceptance of (1) and (2) as conditions on knowledge.

We have seen that Ideal Analysis accepts the following condition on Kap:

(3) $Kap \supset p$.

(3) entails (1) if we allow Kap to stand in the place of p. This is explicitly allowed in most formal treatments of belief operators. (Technically, we have been rather informal. The statement letter p has been taken as abstracting a sentence in past appearances, so we can't substitute for it like we could for a variable. Also, in belief contexts, we did not want to consider unlimited iteration, which is what substitution allows. But since we have treated p as abstracting an arbitrary factual sentence, we can regard it now as a variable and permit

substitution. The technical adjustments required are quite straightforward.) That acceptance of (1) is part of any Ideal Analysis is thus pretty straightforward. More argument is required to see that (2) is a necessary part of the Ideal Analysis. Clearly (2) does not hold if knowledge is construed merely as true belief, since we have seen that (2) fails under various belief readings. For rational belief, however, we can utilize our consistency test to show that $B = \{Bap, \sim BaBap\}$ is inconsistent. Therefore, the following would be a condition on rational belief:

(4) $Bap \supset BaBap$.

(From this formula it is easy to see why substitution would permit unlimited iteration of belief operators.) Suppose we treat knowledge as true rational belief. Then we have this definition:

(5) $Kap \equiv Bap \wedge p$.

Once again, treating p as a statement letter for which we can substitute, we have the following:

(6) $KaKap \equiv Ka(Bap \wedge p)$.

It seems natural to suppose that if someone knows that $(p \wedge q)$, then he knows that p and he knows that q. We will say that the operator Ka distributes over conjunction. Using this distribution property, we turn (6) into (7):

(7) $KaKap \equiv KaBap \wedge Kap$.

By substitution into (5), we get (8):

(8) $KaBap \equiv BaBap \wedge Bap$.

Using (5) and (8) to substitute into (7), we obtain (9):

(9) $KaKap \equiv BaBap \wedge Bap \wedge p.$

Since we already have (1), we are interested in proving (2) given (4). Assume (10):

(10) $Kap.$

From (10) and (5) we obtain (11):

(11) $Bap \wedge p.$

Using (4), we see that (11) implies (12):

(12) $BaBap \wedge Bap \wedge p.$

By (12) and (9), we obtain (13):

(13) $KaKap.$

(10) and (13) therefore provide a conditional proof of (2).

The situation is somewhat more complicated when we admit the justification condition that is required for knowledge on the Ideal Analysis. Let us use Jap to abstract the fact that a's evidence E completely justifies a in believing that p. Then we have this definition:

(14) $Kap \equiv Jap \wedge Bap \wedge p.$

Substituting and simplifying, we obtain the following from (14):

(15) $KaKap \equiv BaBap \wedge JaBap \wedge Bap \wedge BaJap \wedge JaJap \wedge Jap \wedge p.$

If we try a conditional proof of $KaKap$ from Kap as before, it is easy to see that we can prove $\{BaBap, Bap, BaJap, Jap, p\}$ from $\{Bap, Jap, p\}$ using the properties of rational belief. That leaves $JaJap$ and $JaBap$ to be established. If the Ideal Analysis could be shown to involve the following principles, then the Ideal Analysis would definitely involve acceptance of (1) and (2):

(16) $Bap \land Jap \supset JaBap$.

(17) $Jap \supset JaJap$.

(16) says that if a believes that p and p is justified on a's evidence, then a is justified in believing that p. On this reading, (16) seems an assumption required by the Ideal Analysis, or by any reasonable analysis of rational belief. (17) is the tricky one, and it requires careful scrutiny against our intuitions about an acceptable notion of justification. Suppose a is not completely justified in being completely justified that p. This suggests that there is a (non-metaphysical) reason to doubt that p is true, or evidence of some sort counting against the truth of p. But in that case, a cannot be completely justified in believing that p. By contraposition, (17) seems to hold of any rigorous notion of complete justification.

The version of our partial analysis that is compatible with the Ideal Analysis seems to suggest a similar result. Here $KaKap$ is read as "a can meet all possible non-metaphysical objections to his meeting all possible non-metaphysical objections to p." Suppose $KaKap$ false. Then there is some possible non-metaphysical objection to some way in which a meets a possible non-metaphysical objection to p. But this objection must be equivalent to an objection to p which a cannot meet, so Kap is also false. By contraposition, the partial analysis on the strong reading that meshes with an Ideal Analysis involves acceptance of (2).

Is (2) true? Many philosophers have argued that it is false. The arguments that (2) is false often depend on a definition of knowledge that is different from the

Ideal Analysis, or are unconvincing. We give one example of each kind of argument in order to illustrate.

E. J. Lemmon has argued that (2) is false on the grounds of an analysis of knowledge we have not yet considered. Let *Kap* be defined as follows:

(18) *Kap* if and only if a learned that p and a has not forgotten that p.

This analysis is reminiscent of a conception of knowledge at least as old as the one provided in Plato's *Meno*. There Plato argued that since we can't *acquire* knowledge from experience (experience can only give us misleading evidence about changing objects in the world of becoming) we must have had it since before birth. The solution is that the soul (mind) has always known the unchanging Forms that are the object of true knowledge, and a human being can have access to this knowledge if he consults the uncontaminated wisdom of his soul. We have not considered the Platonic tradition here since it seems capable of providing an adequate account (but not the only one) of mathematical knowledge, but not of providing an adequate account of scientific knowledge and matters of everyday fact. Lemmon's definition is somewhat different from Plato's since it apparently permits one to learn things from experience during his lifetime. We will see below, however, that it has at least one important point in common with Plato's definition. Given (18), a knows that he knows that p if and only if he has learned that he knows that p and has not forgotten that he knows that p. We have already met Lemmon's counterexample. Suppose a learns the expansion π to four places and is asked to produce it. At first (10:30) he cannot, and then (10:35) he does. His production of the numbers at 10:35 suggests that he *did* know the expansion at

10:30, but at 10:30 he had apparently forgotten that he had learned the expansion. Given the analysis and these intuitions, at 10:30 *Kap* is true but *KaKap* is false. We have seen previously that rote memory is a limiting case of knowledge, but that point is not important here. Even if Lemmon's case against (2) can be made out, which seems quite doubtful because of prima-facie obscurities connected with the notion of forgetting (failure to consciously remember doesn't show that one has forgotten), it is based on a conception of knowledge quite different from that which we have been pursuing. It also seems to be the case that this is not an interesting total analysis of knowledge. It appears to suffer from vitiating circularity on the surface, since "I learned that *p*" would seem to entail "I knew that *p*." As an analysis of knowledge it therefore won't do the job that the Ideal Analysis has been attacking.

An unconvincing argument against (2) is that if (2) is accepted, then one cannot know without knowing that one knows, and this points toward an infinite regress. Actually, accepting (1) and (2) is accepting the view that knowing that one knows and knowing are the same state, so no regress is involved—just different ways of characterizing the same state.

Is it correct to hold that knowing and knowing that one knows are the same state? It seems quite clear that the general answer to this question is in the negative. A student who has completed some course of instruction may know certain things, in the partially analytic sense that he can now meet all relevant non-metaphysical objections to various claims, but he may not know that he can do this because he is as yet unaware of the objections he can meet when they are posed. Or, if he has heard a great many objections, he may not yet know that he has heard them all, although in fact he has. A man knows when he can meet all of the objections, but he may not know that he can meet all the objections. The reader no doubt senses immediately that although this claim may seem true, it depends on the notion of *all objections to a claim* that previously resulted in two versions of our partial analysis. If "all objections" is read as meaning *all possible relevant non-metaphysical objections,* then (2) is compatible with the Ideal Analysis. This follows from the power of the notion of all possible relevant non-metaphysical objections, among which are included all possible non-metaphysical objections to the manner in which the agent currently meets relevant non-metaphysical objections. On the other hand, if "all objections" is read as meaning *all current relevant non-metaphysical objections,* this problem disappears. A man *may* be able to meet all current relevant non-metaphysical objections to *p* without being able to meet all possible objections. The phrase "current relevant objection" itself now requires some further attention. We do not want to say that an objection is a "current relevant objection" if it would be relevant if it were formulated, since this seems to collapse to the notion of a possible objection. We therefore do not even want the notion of an objection that *could* be currently formulated because of an obscurity in what this notion may entail. We will say that an objection is a current relevant non-metaphysical objection if it is an objection (or is equivalent to an objection) that has already been formulated and is both relevant and non-metaphysical with respect to *p*. Let us return to *a* who is able to meet all current relevant non-metaphysical objections to *p*. That makes *Kap* true in the circumstances on the Pragmatic Analysis. What is the significance of *KaKap?* It means that *a* can meet all current relevant non-metaphysical objections to his meeting all current relevant non-metaphysical objections to p. Suppose all current relevant non-metaphysical objections to p are equivalent to one of three sentences, b, c, or d. Suppose that a can meet any of b, c, or d. Consider the following claim:

> (19) b, c, and d are not the only current relevant non-metaphysical objections to p.

(19) is not an objection to p, so a does not have to meet it for Kap to hold (although Kap holds only if this claim is false). (19) is not a metaphysical claim since we can imagine that a can investigate the truth or falsity of (19). Whether or not it is true is to be determined by canvassing relevant journal articles, other people working on similar claims, and so forth. (19) is a non-metaphysical objection to a's being able to meet all current relevant non-metaphysical objections. Therefore $KaKap$ does not hold unless a can meet (19). If a has not yet carried out the investigation required to meet (19), Kap is true and $KaKap$ is false. The Pragmatic Analysis allows us to retain the intuition that (2) is false. This seems to provide a powerful argument for preferring a Pragmatic Analysis to any form of the Ideal Analysis.

It is useful to compare the Ideal and Pragmatic Analyses with respect to some broad areas of human knowledge. We will make some remarks here about the manner in which they contrast with respect to mathematical knowledge, scientific knowledge (empirical as opposed to mathematical), and everyday matters of fact. The general result of these comparisons is that the Ideal and Pragmatic Analyses most clearly resemble one another in the case of mathematical knowledge, are in reasonably close agreement in at least some cases of scientific knowledge, and diverge rather sharply in the case of everyday matters of fact. If the existence and differences between the analyses are not noticed in the mathematical and scientific cases, there is a potential error to be realized in fitting the Ideal Analysis to these cases, and then attempting to extend it to everyday matters of fact, where it seems not to fit. This error is of interest in that it seems to be frequently realized in the literature. Since the Pragmatic Analysis will fit all three cases, it seems correct to view the concepts of scientific and mathematical knowledge as having arisen from more pedestrian instances of human knowledge, and to regard the Ideal Analysis as an idealization of the Pragmatic Analysis which fits the facts of scientific and mathematical knowledge just as well as the Pragmatic Analysis but offers some attractive features for analyzing these more special cases. Our survey of this situation will of necessity be compressed. The reader is invited to elaborate and revise the general outlines of this survey in accordance with his own intuitions about mathematics, science, and everyday affairs.

The facts about mathematical knowledge of interest to us are independent of the question whether the objects of mathematical knowledge are given a Platonic construal or a construal as conventional objects postulated by human conceptual processes. We start with the following observation. In many mathematical contexts, the denial of a mathematical claim is an alternative mathematical claim. For example, given the existence of some twin primes (successive odd numbers both of which are prime, for example 107 and 109), and their decreasing frequency as the integers get larger, we have only two hypotheses: There is a greatest pair of twin primes, and there is no greatest pair of twin primes.

Let p and $\sim p$ stand for such a pair of alternative hypotheses in an appropriate context. Most mathematicians have accepted that, say, p is known to be true provided that $\sim p$ can be refuted. (A statement abstracted to $\sim p$ is known to be true if p can be refuted.) An accepted procedure where this refutation will work is to assume $\sim p$, deduce a contradiction showing $\sim p$ to be false, and hence conclude that p is true by application of the Law of Excluded Middle from Standard Logic. In cases such as this, provided that the *reductio* proof is accepted, we see an instance where the Ideal Analysis and the Pragmatic Analysis are identical in application. A statement abstracted to $\sim p$ is always a current relevant non-metaphysical objection to p, and in contexts as simple as that already supposed, it is the only possible relevant non-metaphysical objection to p. In many mathematical contexts, therefore, the class of current objections to a hypothesis is identical with the class of possible objections, and the two analyses of knowledge coincide. It is only necessary to point out that there are many such cases in mathematics to see why the Ideal and Pragmatic Analyses are not likely to be distinguished if one takes classical mathematical knowledge as the sole paradigm of human knowledge.

This brisk treatment of mathematical knowledge would require considerable elaboration in the face of various complexities. Two such complexities will be mentioned here. It has happened many times in the history of mathematics that the class of current objections to a mathematical hypothesis did not exhaust the retrospective class of possible objections. Historical discoveries, like those of complex numbers and non-Euclidean geometries, have increased the range of various possible alternative mathematical hypotheses. This is true, but it can be misunderstood. The *range* that is increased is typically that of the variety of mathematical *systems*. Older systems are then qualified in a manner that preserves the already discovered truth of their hypotheses. Before the discovery of non-Euclidean geometries, *geometry* was simply what we now consider *Euclidean geometry*. After the discovery of non-Euclidean geometry, the theses of Euclidean geometry did not become false because alternative theses (in another system) were true. It was, however, necessary to qualify the theses explicitly as theses of Euclidean geometry. Instead of saying, "The sum of the interior angles of a triangle is 180°," one then had to say, "The sum of the interior angles of a Euclidean plane triangle is 180°." Indeed, by remembering that one is working within Euclidean geometry, it was not necessary to change the statement of the theses at all. The evolution of new mathematical systems does not, therefore, seem to seriously threaten the claim that in a wide range of cases, the class of current objections to a mathematical hypothesis and the class of possible objections to the same hypothesis can be regarded as equivalent.

The other complexity to be mentioned here is the claim by constructivists or intuitionists that the classical *reductio* proof is not valid because, for example, both p and $\sim p$ may be mathematical nonsense. Intuitionists are likely to find nonsense in claims made about infinite collections whose members cannot be generated by certain sorts of recursive processes. If p and $\sim p$ can both be nonsense, then a *reductio* of $\sim p$ would hardly establish p. The intuitionists suggest as an Ideal Analysis of mathematical knowledge something like this: a knows that p if and only if p can be derived from a finite set of intuitionistically acceptable sentences by a finite number of applications of intuitionistically acceptable rules of inference. This obviously has the pattern of an analysis of knowledge into basic knowledge (intuitionistically acceptable premises) plus deductive inference (of a rigorously specified sort) from basic knowledge. The existence of basic knowledge and acceptable rules is *not* stipulative, since in a mathematical context they can be listed (and *are* listed) by the intuitionists. Clearly, the motivation of the intuitionists is conservative. Once an item of mathematical knowledge is constructively established, it should remain an item of mathematical knowledge. Knowledge should be built so carefully that it is not necessary to repair errors in previous mathematical proofs. The relationship between constructivists or intuitionists and other philosophical mathematicians is roughly this: All intuitionistic results are acceptable to other mathematicians, but as we have seen, there are commonly accepted mathematical results that are not intuitionistically acceptable. For our purposes, it is not necessary to resolve issues in the philosophy of mathematics. What intuitionistic programs show is that there are areas of knowledge where the Ideal Analysis and the Pragmatic Analysis are indistinguishable in practice. They also show that there are areas of knowledge in which a distinction like that between basic and derived knowledge is observed. These facts mean that it would be wrong to offer any blanket condemnation of the Ideal Analysis. It fits at least the important case of broad areas (if not all) of pure mathematics. Our question now is how Pragmatic and Ideal Analyses compare in other areas where human knowledge is claimed.

The connection between Ideal and Pragmatic Analyses of knowledge and the facts of scientific knowledge is considerably simplified if one accepts the notion that there is a single methodology for science. Many philosophers have accepted the idea of a single methodology under the concept of some unified science hypothesis. The methodology invoked by unified science hypotheses has nearly always been abstracted from classical physics. Classical physics and the resultant abstracted methodology have some interesting properties that make it fairly plausible that an Ideal Analysis of knowledge is applicable. For example, the claims of classical physics often involve the properties of individual particles (electrons, for example) that exist in huge classes all of the members of which are theoretically identical (all electrons have the same charge, for example). This property of classical physics has the result that statistical sampling is an ideal model for experimental data. The inductive inference from properties of the particles with which one is experimenting to the whole population is not very risky because one can assume that one's sample population is not biased. In theory, philosophers of science have pointed out that one might have to postulate the irrelevance of spatio-temporal position to physical properties of the experiment, and so forth, if one is to have a logically acceptable account of experimental method. But these postulations are clearly minor tidying operations in a picture whose gross features are intuitively acceptable. It should particularly be noted that an experimenter could typically "prepare" the particles of his experiment so as to obtain them in a pure state, and could control the environment so as to influence the particles with just those factors that were of theoretical interest. In classical circumstances, only the barest rift between Ideal and Practical Analyses of knowledge is discernible. Current objections might not exhaust possible objections because of unknown physical factors, but the repeatability of experiments gives good grounds for thinking that the relevant factors are all accounted for. There is every philosophical justification for thinking that a *careful description* of the classical experimental situation could exclude unknown possible objections—and, therefore, the Ideal Analysis seems both to apply and to be right because of the close link between statistical experimental models and the notion of complete justification. As a result, either the Ideal Analysis or the Pragmatic Analysis can be regarded as fitting the facts. It might even be suggested that justified true belief is a good analysis of a wide range of scientific examples of knowledge. Certainly the Gettier counterexamples are hard to work out in this context. Let the scientist make a controlled experiment on a group of prepared particles. It's pointless to suggest that his actual measurements might be in error and the result incorrect. This is a feature that ongoing experiment is designed to handle. In the meantime, the result stands as part of scientific knowledge. Again, it is difficult to destroy the relevance of the evidence due to the controlled nature of the work. It doesn't matter if a few particles get exchanged—they're all identical anyway. Could the whole nature of the universe be changing, so that the knowledge gained from the experiment will not be valid for the future? Such doubts remain metaphysical unless a specific reason for thinking them true can arise. On balance, then, the justified true belief style of analysis seems an acceptable analysis of the knowledge derived from classical physical theory.

As one moves from classical physics to areas of science that are perhaps not reducible to physics (such as broad areas of biology) this simple picture evaporates. Scientific knowledge begins to look methodologically akin to matters of everyday fact. It should be remembered in this connection that there are useful generalizations in plumbing, in cooking, and in many activities not usually regarded as sciences. In large areas of science, and in everyday matters of fact, the split between possible and current objections is nearly obvious. People working in these scientific areas and ordinary people in everyday quandaries *know* that they don't command all possible objections because they cannot explain and control that which they feel is subject to some sort of deeper understanding than they have. Nonetheless, books about what is known in these areas are written and consumed. If we stick with the Ideal Analysis, they must all be consigned equally to the flames. We might note that the Gettier counterexamples arise precisely in this area and they are telling partly because of the fact that we have observed failure of relevance of good evidence in the past. There is even a sense in which the Gettier counterexamples are themselves either metaphysical objections to possible situations or are convincing because the Pragmatic Analysis is correct. Let us go back to Jones and the example where *a* believes (falsely) that Jones owns a Ford. Jones presumably knows that he doesn't own a Ford, so there is an actual current objection to *a*'s knowledge claim that *a* can't meet. A Gettier counterexample of this kind is then quite compatible with the Pragmatic Analysis while telling against the Ideal Analysis of the same situation. On the other hand, the extended sense in which Gettier counterexamples can be developed to show failure of relevance against abstract situations yields metaphysical objections only if someone has a reason to think such a failure of relevance is occurring, in which case the Pragmatic Analysis explains why we want to say that knowledge has not been attained.

Summarizing our survey of cases, the following points should be made. In matters of everyday fact, and perhaps in many areas of science, the Pragmatic Analysis seems to fit the facts while the Ideal Analysis apparently entails a form of skepticism. In other areas of science (at least those having a structure fitting the classical methodology of unified science) and in mathematics, either the Ideal Analysis or the Pragmatic Analysis seem to fit the facts because of the conflation of the notions of *possible objection* and *current objection*. One conclusion seems to be that the Pragmatic Analysis should be regarded as the more basic of the two, while the Ideal Analysis can be regarded as a deeper, more general philosophical analysis of great value in restricted circumstances where relevance is assured by the structure of the subject matter. The Pragmatic Analysis is not general in the sense that *current relevant non-metaphysical objection* is highly dependent contextually. To find out whether someone knows something, we need to find out how he came to believe that he knew it. In everyday cases, the situation is settled partly by convention, partly by our natural history. Having seen something is generally better than having been told about it, and so forth. In the scientific cases, however, we need to discover the state of the art if we don't already know it. The current controversies and experimental results must be mastered. It is because of this that the Pragmatic Analysis, while a general *characterization* of knowledge, is highly contextually dependent in application. The Pragmatic Analysis may thus appear unsatisfactory to many. What needs to be thought about is whether the Pragmatic Analysis doesn't yield really all that can be said about knowledge in many contexts. Should that be so, it will appear in retrospect that a lot of the emotional heat in the philosophical controversies about the nature of knowledge have been generated by a mistaken attempt to apply the standards of Ideal Analysis to cases which it conceptually cannot fit.

It is appropriate that this study should leave many questions unanswered. We have seen that even such basic questions as necessary and sufficient conditions for the consistency of belief and the existence of knowledge still go without completely satisfactory answers in spite of intensive philosophical investigation. In addition, there are many relatively unexplored presuppositions of the partial answers we have examined which may repay critical scrutiny. Is it the case that *all* of a man's beliefs must be regarded on equal footing at any given time in a consistency test, or is it possible that consistent belief is contextually dependent, in the sense that beliefs are clustered into groups of beliefs only one group (or a few groups) of which may be activated in connection with a given problem or situation—so that apparently inconsistent beliefs may be no more inconsistent than apparently contradictory theses embedded in two different systems? Can rationality be attacked in terms of the structure of belief and knowledge in an individual at a time? Or should rationality be regarded as a dynamic feature of human beings that is best instanced in the way their beliefs and knowledge claims adapt to new situations over a period of time, a view that is quite compatible with a rational man relying on "guess" or "hunch" or "insight" in violation of likelihood notions of rationality in circumstances where insufficient information is available. It has even been suggested that the creative process (in science as elsewhere) is stimulated by perceived inconsistency, so that a person with a difficult problem may try to heighten inconsistent aspects of it in order to look for a solution. These sorts of considerations point to deep problems with which contemporary philosophers have as yet hardly concerned themselves. In this study, we have examined some of the views about belief and knowledge that have been current in the last decade. The philosophers who have struggled with these views and with the questions we have raised are perhaps those most acutely aware of what remains to be done.

Appendix

Opacity of Belief and Knowledge Constructions

In Chapter 2, we pointed out that while the hyphenating policy is conservative with respect to inference, it does not capture relevant aspects of the form of various sentences having belief constructions. A related problem arises for sentences having knowledge constructions. There are a number of problems concerning belief and knowledge that are too sophisticated for inclusion in the text. A few of these problems will be barely introduced here along with a few references for the reader who finds them interesting. The sort of problem that requires attention can be illustrated by a set of examples:

(1) Tom believes that someone is a spy.
(2) There is someone such that Tom believes that he is a spy.
(3) Tom knows that someone is a spy.
(4) There is someone such that Tom knows that he is a spy.

It is interesting to consider circumstances in which (1) and (2) are appropriate. (1) might be appropriate if Tom notices that top secret documents are missing, so that he merely believes that there is a spy. (2) seems appropriate if Tom suspects someone (say Harry) of being a spy but has no conclusive evidence. (3) and (4) can be distinguished by related scenarios. These scenarios also show that (1) can be true while (2) is

false, and that (3) can be true while (4) is false. It is
also tempting to suppose, given the scenarios, that (2)
entails (1) and that (4) entails (3). Using the hyphenating policy, (1) and (3) might be abstracted to (5)
and (6), respectively:

(5) $B't$.
(6) $K't$.

(2) and (4) would have to be abstracted to something
like (7) and (8):

(7) $B'\,'t$.
(8) $K'\,'t$.

To have entailments, we would have to introduce postu-
lates to connect specific pairs of beliefs. For example, if
(2) entails (1) no matter what name is substituted for
Tom in both, we could have a postulate like (9) as
part of a formalization of English:

(9) $(x)(B'\,'x \supset B'x)$.

The hyphenating policy is inadequate here as elsewhere.
It simply does not allow us to represent in any perspicuous fashion the relationship of form that we find between (2) and (1).

Using Predicate Logic in a straightforward but naïve
way, we could abstract (1)–(4) to the following
formulae:

(10) $Bt(\exists x)(Sx)$.
(11) $(\exists x)(BtSx)$.
(12) $Kt(\exists x)(Sx)$.
(13) $(\exists x)(KtSx)$.

The difficulty here is in interpreting (6) and (8). Let
us go back to our scenario. Tom discovers top secret
documents missing. Tom believes in the circumstances

that the man who took the documents is a spy. Let b equal the man who took the documents. We then, apparently, have a true claim that can be abstracted to (14):

(14) $BtSb$.

The problem is how to permit inference to (10) without allowing inference to (11).

The position of W. V. O. Quine is that this cannot be done. If b occurs in (14) in a location that can be quantified, then it occurs in a location where substitution can occur according to the laws of identity. Now we might try using a rule to the effect that existential quantification is to be introduced with the smallest possible scope of the quantifier. Then we can get (10) from (14) but not (11) by this rule. However, let Harry be the man who took the documents, and let h equal Harry. We have (15) as a true identity:

(15) $h = b$.

On Quine's reading, if (14) can give us (10) because b occurs in a referential position in (14), then we can get the following from (14) and (15):

(16) $BtSh$.

(16), however, is a formula that seems equivalent to the belief that authorized (2). Therefore, we should be able to derive (11) from (16). A similar line of reasoning shows that if we can obtain (12) in a suitable scenario, we can also use a true identity to derive (13). Using a standard reading in Predicate Logic of the formulae (10)–(13), therefore, we can't seem to find an interpretation that satisfies our original intuitions that in the proper scenario (1) might be true while (2) is false. If keeping Standard Logic then takes precedence over other possible courses of action, one may conclude that quantification cannot coherently be used as a total analysis of epistemic sentences where it is used in such a fashion that its scope coincides with the scope of belief and knowledge operators. Quine's original views can be found in sections 35 and 41–45 of *Word and Object* (Wiley, New York, 1960). Some modifications and changes in Quine's views brought about by recent work in Non-Standard Logic are to be found by consulting the essays by Dagfinn Føllesdal, Wilfrid Sellars, and David Kaplan along with Quine's replies to these essays in Donald Davidson and Jaakko Hintikka (eds.), *Words and Objections: Essays on the Work of W. V. Quine* (Reidel, Dordrecht, and Humanities, New York, 1969).

The other obvious move in response to the problems raised by our examples, but which is motivated by a desire to preserve the distinctions that intuition suggests to us, is to try to develop some form of Non-Standard Logic in which the significance of names or of quantification is construed somewhat differently than in Standard Logic. Here, Jaakko Hintikka is the major figure. Hintikka's system in *Knowledge and Belief* (Cornell, Ithaca, 1962) involves the use of a quantified modal logic that attempts to develop various senses in which a person may be said to recognize another. The problem can be set by an example:

(17) She believed that my brother was deliberately rude.

There are at least two important but different claims that this sentence can be used to make. In the one claim, some behavior of one's brother was taken by the lady in question to be deliberately rude in circumstances where the lady knew and recognized one's brother as the bad actor. On some other occasion, one's brother might be taken as rude by a lady to whom one's brother was a complete stranger. Although in this case one could use (17) to report what happened, the lady in question could not have said, "Your brother was deliberately rude," to the speaker later reporting events. We would, therefore, expect that in a suitable logic for belief, these two readings of (17) would be captured by divergent formulae, each of which would have (some) different formulae as consequences. This suggests that the role of names in belief and knowledge contexts needs to be treated differently, and so also the related notion of quantification. Otherwise, one is left with Quine's position or with a program of attempting to work out a logic of propositions, individual concepts, or some such entities. Looking back at our example, since Tom recognizes Harry *as* Harry, but can't recognize the man who took the documents *as* the man who took the documents (when he sees him he doesn't recognize him as the spy), we would expect that the counterparts of (14) and (16) in a suitable quantified modal logic would not differ merely in an occurrence of a name. It would then be possible to keep identity theory intact but permit derivation of a counterpart for (10) from the counterpart formula of (14) and derivation of a counterpart for (11) from the counterpart formula of (16) while in some situations the counterpart of (14) is true and that of (16) is false. Space limitations preclude a coherent introduction to non-standard interpretations of names or quantifiers here. There have been many attempts to construct logics using special names or other ways of representing individual concepts and propositions in logics suitable for expressing the form of epistemic statements. We mention here some of the current literature that has drawn wide attention. The reader should also consult Further Reading for some other suggestions about related matters. Jaakko Hintikka, *Knowledge and Belief* (Cornell, Ithaca, 1962) is the contemporary classic. See Further Reading, Chapter 2, for references to some critical literature about *Knowledge and Belief*. Hintikka's current position is outlined in his paper, "Objects of Knowledge and Belief: Acquaintances and Public Figures," *The Journal of Philosophy 67* (1970), pp. 869–83. An approach considerably different from Hintikka's is developed by David Kaplan in his important paper, "Quantifying In," in Donald Davidson and Jaakko Hintikka, eds., *Words and Objections: Essays on the Work of W. V. O. Quine* (Reidel, Dordrecht, and Humanities, New York, 1969), pp. 206–42. Wilfrid Sellars utilizes individual concepts in his system of representation. See Wilfrid Sellars, "Some Problems about Belief," in Davidson and Hintikka eds., *op. cit.,* pp. 186–205. Discussion of Hintikka, Kaplan, and Sellars, as well as of the recent work of Castañeda, Chisholm, Schwartz, and others, is to be found in Ernest Sosa, "Propositional Attitudes *de Dictu* and *de Re,*" *The Journal of Philosophy 67* (1970), pp. 883–96.

Further Reading

This monograph is intended for a student of philosophy who is not yet familiar with any of the technical philosophical literature about belief and knowledge. In order to make the monograph as readable as possible, footnotes have been ruthlessly suppressed, partly because full documentation of the ideas of various authors that are alluded to in the text would involve enormous and distracting bibliographical apparatus. No full references are even possible, since in an area of burgeoning research, many of the current ideas exist in personal correspondence or in the context of discussions at various meetings. In this section, I offer some highly personalized suggestions to the reader about continuing investigation of any topic he finds interesting. A reader who turns to the sources suggested will find himself immersed in the actual literature, and by consulting, in turn, the literature cited in these sources, he will find ready access to everything that is worth reading about these matters.

Chapter 1

The kinds of belief distinguished in this chapter are a reflection of subtle hints in the literature. In actual fact, there are few papers by philosophers that are not about conscious belief or rational belief in the sense of the chapter. A notable exception is Arthur W. Collins,

"Unconscious Belief," *The Journal of Philosophy* 66 (1969), pp. 667–80. This article is a useful survey of the facts that must be considered in distinguishing unconscious belief from various forms of conscious belief. Discussions of the properties of conscious and rational belief will be found in the literature mentioned in connection with Chapter 2.

Chapter 2

The hyphenating policy appears to be explicitly stated infrequently in the Procrustean form described in the text. One hears it advanced frequently in discussion, or proposed as a view that is largely correct. For example, consider the following quotation from W. V. O. Quine, *Word and Object* (Wiley, New York, 1960), p. 216:

> Hence a final alternative that I find as appealing as any is simply to dispense with the objects of the propositional attitudes. . . . This means viewing "Tom believes [Cicero denounced Cataline]" no longer as of the form "*Fab*" with $a =$ Tom and $b =$ [Cicero denounced Cataline], but rather as of the form "*Fa*" with $a =$ Tom and complex "*F*."

This quotation is perhaps not fair to the power and complexity of Quine's exploration of belief sentences, but a student interested in the pressures leading to some version of the hyphenating policy could do no better than to study *Word and Object*. The objection mentioned in the text that some version of the hyphenating policy would render language unlearnable is explored in Donald Davidson, "Theories of Meaning and Learnable Languages," in Bar-Hillel, ed., *Proceedings of the 1964 International Congress for Logic, Methodology, and Philosophy of Science* (North-Holland,

Amsterdam, and Humanities, New York, 1965), pp. 383–94.

Behavioral analyses of belief are critically examined in Chapter Four of Israel Scheffler's *Conditions of Knowledge* (Scott, Foresman & Co., Chicago, 1965). Relational analyses involving propositions are discussed extensively by W. V. O. Quine, for example, in sections 35 and 41 of *Word and Object*. Quine's objections to the notion of possibility required to explicate propositional identity have recently been attacked by works of Kripke, Hintikka, and Montague. See Jaakko Hintikka, *Models for Modalities* (Reidel, Dordrecht, and Humanities, New York, 1969) and Richard Montague, "On the Nature of Certain Philosophical Entities," *The Monist 53* (1969), pp. 159–94. For an interesting survey of various philosophical positions about belief, followed by an extremely interesting suggestion about the grammar of belief sentences, see Murray Kiteley, "The Grammars of 'Believe,'" *The Journal of Philosophy 61* (1964), pp. 244–59.

Jaakko Hintikka has provided the focus for contemporary discussions of the consistency of belief and knowledge with the system he introduces in *Knowledge and Belief* (Cornell, Ithaca, 1962). The test for consistency introduced in this chapter is a modified version of Hintikka's test in cases where only Propositional Logic is used to expose the logical form of belief sentences and where there is limited iteration of belief operators. Hintikka's full system uses Predicate Logic, and the theorems of the extended system have generated a lot of controversy. See discussion in papers by Castañeda, Chisholm, Sleigh, and Hintikka in *Nous 1* (1967), pp. 1–62; papers by Sleigh and Stine in subsequent issues of *Nous;* papers by Sellars and Sosa in Davis, Hockney, and Wilson, eds., *Philosophical Logic*

(Reidel, Dordrecht, and Humanities, New York, 1969); a paper by Swain in Marshall Swain, ed., *Induction, Acceptance, and Rational Belief* (Reidel, Dordrecht, and Humanities, New York, 1970); papers by Hilpinen, Castañeda, Ginet, and Hintikka in *Synthese 21* (June 1970); and papers by Hintikka and Sosa in *The Journal of Philosophy 67* (1970), pp. 841-69.

Chapter 3

Basic issues about consistency, coherence, and rational belief can be examined in a series of useful papers by Frederic Schick. See "Consistency and Rationality," *The Journal of Philosophy 60* (1963), pp. 5-19; "Consistency," *The Philosophical Review 75* (1966), pp. 467-95; and in Marshall Swain, ed., "Three Logics of Belief," *Induction, Acceptance, and Rational Belief* (Reidel, Dordrecht, and Humanities, New York, 1970), pp. 6-26. Schick's papers examine the lottery paradox and solutions to it in much greater detail than is possible in this monograph. An interesting discussion of Schick's paper "Consistency" is to be found in Ronald DeSousa's paper "Consistent Belief," read at the Western Division Meetings of the American Philosophical Association in 1970. This paper is currently unpublished, but information about it may be available from DeSousa at the University of Toronto.

The lottery paradox was first formulated by Henry E. Kyburg, Jr., who developed a theory of belief to circumvent it. Kyburg's theory utilizes the first strategy mentioned in this text, but it was not adequate in its original formulation. (See Schick, "Consistency and Rationality," *op. cit.*) Kyburg's justification for rejecting the deductivity assumption and his current strategy for avoiding the lottery paradox are explored in his article "Conjunctivitis," in Marshall Swain, ed., *Induction, Acceptance, and Rational Belief* (Reidel, Dordrecht, and Humanities, New York, 1970), pp. 55–82.

Partial belief theories are widely held by philosophers and by some statisticians. A classical version of a partial belief theory with a likelihood assumption is that of Rudolf Carnap. There is a brief introduction and a discussion of some criticisms in Robert Ackermann, *Nondeductive Inference* (Routledge, London, 1966). Carnap's classic is *Logical Foundations of Probability* (Chicago University Press, Chicago, 1950). Because of changes in the system (more correctly, changes in the set of systems) and in the motivation, it is useful to look at Kemeny's article, pp. 711–39, and at Carnap's "Replies and Systematic Expositions," pp. 859–1017 of P. A. Schilpp, ed., *The Philosophy of Rudolf Carnap* (Open Court, La Salle, Illinois, 1963). Partial belief theories without a likelihood assumption are closely akin to modern subjectivistic theories of statistical inference and decision making as developed by F. P. Ramsay, Bruno DeFinetti, and L. J. Savage. See Ackermann, *op. cit.* for a brief introduction and suggestions about further reading. A highly recommended philosophical treatment is provided by R. C. Jeffrey in *The Logic of Decision* (McGraw-Hill, New York, 1965).

The third strategy for avoiding the lottery paradox is presented by Isaac Levi in his book *Gambling With Truth* (Knopf, New York, 1967). Jeffrey and Levi are perhaps the leading spokesmen for the second and third strategies introduced in the text. The arguments for and against these two positions can be traced in a series of polemical articles between Jeffrey and Levi. A late installment is to be found in their papers (and references) in Marshall Swain, ed., *Induction, Acceptance, and Rational Belief* (Reidel, Dordrecht, and Humanities, New York, 1970), pp. 134–85. A very full bibliography for all of the topics in Chapter 3 is provided by Ralph L. Slaght on pp. 186–227 of the same volume.

Chapter 4

Most of the grammatical observations about knowledge and belief in this chapter are the coin of the realm, so to speak, and they appear scattered about in the literature. Many of them are reviewed in Israel Scheffler, *Conditions of Knowledge* (Scott, Foresman, Chicago, 1965), especially Chapters 1 and 5. Some examples of knowledge from ordinary contexts are provided by Colin Radford in "Knowledge by Examples," *Analysis* 27 (1966), pp. 1–11. DeSousa's example appears on p. 71 of Ronald DeSousa, "Knowledge, Consistent Belief, and Self-Consciousness," *The Journal of Philosophy* 67 (1970), pp. 66–73. Knowledge of one's own pains has a famous recent history because of the connection between this problem and the so-called Private Language Argument associated with Ludwig Wittgenstein's *Philosophical Investigations*. Should there be a reader who has not heard about this, it might prove sufficient to look at John W. Cook, "Wittgenstein on Privacy," *The Philosophical Review 74* (1965), pp. 281–314. Cook's article is reprinted along with other papers on the same topic in George Pitcher, ed., *Wittgenstein* (Anchor Books, New York, 1966). The distinction between *knowing how* and *knowing that* has played an important role in modern philosophy. There is considerable well-known discussion in Gilbert Ryle, *The Concept of Mind* (Hutchinson, London, and

Barnes & Noble, New York, 1949). For a recent critical discussion of the distinction, see D. G. Brown, "Knowing How and Knowing That, What," in Oscar P. Wood and George Pitcher, eds., *Ryle* (Anchor Books, New York, 1970), pp. 213–49.

Chapter 5

Gettier counterexamples arise from the pair presented by Gettier in Edmund L. Gettier, "Is Justified True Belief Knowledge?" *Analysis 23* (1963), pp. 121–23. This was followed by a series of articles discussing Gettier's paper: Michael Clark, "Knowledge and Grounds: A Comment on Gettier's Paper," *Analysis 24* (1964), pp. 46–47; John Turk Saunders and Narayan Champawat, "Mr. Clark's Definition of 'Knowledge,'" *Analysis 25* (1965), pp. 8–9; Ernest Sosa, "The Analysis of 'Knowledge that *P*,'" *Analysis 25* (1965), pp. 1–3; and Keith Lehrer, "Knowledge, Truth, and Evidence," *Analysis 25* (1965), pp. 168–75.

The principles of complete justification used in Gettier counterexamples are usually accepted. For criticism, however, see Irving Thalberg, "In Defense of Justified True Belief," *The Journal of Philosophy 66* (1969), pp. 794–803. Thalberg points out the implicit use of this principle in the simple Gettier counterexamples. A more sustained argument against the principles can be found in Fred I. Dretske, "Epistemic Operators," *The Journal of Philosophy 67* (1970), pp. 1007–23.

An example where s entails t and new evidence is given that lowers the likelihood of t while raising that of s is given by Rudolf Carnap, *Logical Foundations of Probability* (Chicago, 1950), pp. 395–97. (See

Carnap's Index under "Special Consequence Condition" for other references.) Carnap's example is roughly this. Ten players compete in a chess tournament. Some are local players, and some are from the big city. Among junior players, there is one local man, two local women, and two big city men. Among senior players, there are two local men, and three big city women. Let all of the players have an equal chance of winning. On a simple probability model, the likelihood of someone from the big city winning is 5/10. The likelihood of someone from the big city or a senior player winning is 7/10. Let the former claim be s and the latter claim t. Then s entails t since every big city player is either a big city player or a senior. Suppose it is learned that a woman has won. Then the likelihood of s on this information is 6/10 and so is the likelihood of t also 6/10.

Gilbert Harman's suggestions are elaborated in a series of articles the latest of which is Gilbert Harman, "Knowledge, Reasons, and Causes," *The Journal of Philosophy* 67 (1970), pp. 841–55. Two earlier articles may prove helpful in understanding this one. See "Knowledge, Inference, and Explanation," *American Philosophical Quarterly* 5 (1968), pp. 164–73 and "Induction. A Discussion of the Relevance of the Theory of Knowledge to the Theory of Induction (with a Digression to the Effect that neither Deductive Logic nor the Probability Calculus has Anything to Do with Inference)," in Marshall Swain, ed., *Induction, Acceptance, and Rational Belief* (Reidel, Dordrecht, and Humanities, New York, 1970), pp. 83–100.

The suggestion that justified true belief is defeated as knowledge only in circumstances where the agent would be completely justified in believing false that which would defeat his claim was developed in detail by Lehrer and Paxon in Keith Lehrer and Thomas Paxon, Jr., "Knowledge: Undefeated Justified True Belief," *The Journal of Philosophy* 66 (1969), pp. 225–37. The Lehrer and Paxon proposal is shown to be defective in Ernest Sosa, "Two Conceptions of Knowledge," *The Journal of Philosophy* 67 (1970), pp. 59–66. The Lehrer and Paxon article utilizes the distinction between basic knowledge and non-basic knowledge which, in turn, is apparently due to Arthur Danto. See Arthur Danto, *Analytical Philosophy of Knowledge* (Cambridge University, Cambridge and New York, 1968), especially Chapter 2.

The suggestion that one's evidence can only yield knowledge if it justifies only what is true, is elaborated very explicitly by Roderick M. Chisholm in his paper, "On the Nature of Empirical Evidence," in Lawrence Foster and J. W. Swanson, eds., *Experience and Theory* (University of Massachusetts Press, Amherst, 1970). Edmund L. Gettier of the University of Massachusetts has prepared some unpublished criticisms of Chisholm's definitions. Fred Feldman (also of the University of Massachusetts) has offered criticisms which are incorporated into Gettier's paper. A position somewhat related to Chisholm's in its intuitive basis is that of Ernest Sosa. See Ernest Sosa, "Propositional Knowledge," *Philosophical Studies 20* (1969), pp. 33–43, and "Two Conceptions of Knowledge," *The Journal of Philosophy* 67 (1970), pp. 59–66. In the latter paper, Sosa discusses (without solving) various problems with the definitions proposed in the first paper.

Causal analyses have been presented by a number of philosophers. In particular, see the clear presentation by Alvin I. Goldman, "A Causal Theory of Knowing," *The Journal of Philosophy* 64 (1967), pp. 357–72. For a criticism, see Brian Skyrms, "The Explica-

tion of '*X* Knows That *p,*' " *The Journal of Philosophy*
64 (1967), pp. 373–89. Skyrms' article contains many
interesting suggestions for a positive analysis along with
a budget of counterexamples against earlier proposals.

Chapter 6

The style of proof used early in the chapter is derived from Risto Hilpinen, "Knowing that One Knows
and the Classical Definition of Knowledge," *Synthese*
21 (1970), pp. 109–32, and E. J. Lemmon, "If I Know,
Do I Know That I Know?," in Avrum Stroll, ed.,
Epistemology (Harper and Row, New York, 1967),
pp. 54–82. Lemmon's article also contains the discussion of the definition cited in the text.

On knowing that one knows, see the papers in the
June, 1970, issue of *Synthese*. This issue of *Synthese*
contains a Symposium on the topic. Papers by Hilpinen,
Lehrer, Hintikka, Ginet, and Castañeda are included.
Papers by Danto and Lemmon in Stroll, *Epistemology*
(see last paragraph) also deal with this topic. Of these
papers, the paper by Hintikka in the June, 1970 issue
of *Synthese* is absolutely crucial. The system presented
in Hintikka's *Knowledge and Belief* incorporates *Kap*
⊃ *KaKap* as a thesis. Hintikka's defense of *Knowledge
and Belief* in this paper is important because it helps
to clarify the intuitive basis (an Ideal Analysis) for the
system of *Knowledge and Belief*. A related paper of
Hintikka's that should also be studied is "Epistemic
Logic and the Methods of Philosophical Analysis," in
his *Models for Modalities* (Reidel, Dordrecht, and
Humanities, New York, 1969), pp. 3–19.

A proposal that justified true belief theories are an
appropriate technical epistemology suitable for many
scientific contexts is given in William W. Rozeboom,

"Why I Know So Much More Than You Do," *American Philosophical Quarterly 4* (1967), pp. 281–90. Some of the questions raised about belief structures in the last paragraph of the text appear in Howard Darmstadter's interesting paper, "Consistency of Belief," *The Journal of Philosophy 68* (1970), pp. 301–10. Psychologists have made some studies of inconsistent belief. See, for example, Shel Feldman, ed., *Cognitive Consistency* (Academic, New York, 1966) and Milton Rokeach, *Beliefs, Attitudes, and Values* (Jossey-Bass, San Francisco, 1968). In previous publications, the author has discussed a few of these issues. See Robert Ackermann, *Philosophy of Science* (Pegasus, New York, 1970) and "Explanations of Human Action," *Dialogue 6* (1967), pp. 18–28.

Retrospective

This monograph has dealt basically with a cluster of contemporary issues in knowledge and belief, and rather technical issues at that. General questions about the theory of knowledge are broached in many books, for example in D. W. Hamlyn, *The Theory of Knowledge* (Anchor, New York, 1970). For the issues raised in this book, the important contemporary figure is Jaakko Hintikka. The reader who wishes to pursue the issues raised in this monograph is urged to turn to Hintikka's *Knowledge and Belief* and *Models for Modalities* along with the other literature related to these books, which is cited above. It will be seen that Hintikka proposes a form of Ideal Analysis and that he explores it carefully and at an interesting level of detail. Hintikka's system is currently the model against which other proposals need to be tested. For the other literature from journals cited above, the reader who does not have access to specialized philosophical journals can obtain any number of books that reprint most of the essential literature. An example is Michael D. Roth and Leon Galis, eds., *Knowing* (Random House, New York, 1970). Of the papers not likely to be anthologized in such a collection, the author has found the following particularly stimulating: Arthur W. Collins, "Unconscious Belief," *The Journal of Philosophy 66* (1969), pp. 667–80; Howard Darmstadter, *The Journal of Philosophy 68* (1970), pp. 301–10; Gilbert Harman, "Knowledge, Reason, and Causes," *The Journal of Philosophy 67* (1970), pp. 841–55; Murray Kiteley, "The Grammars of 'Believe,'" *The Journal of Philosophy 61* (1964), pp. 244–59; and Frederic Schick, "Consistency and Rationality," *The Journal of Philosophy 60* (1963), pp. 5–19.

BIBLIOGRAPHY

Ackermann, Robert. "Explanations of Human Action," *Dialogue 6* (1967), pp. 18–28.

—— *Nondeductive Inference*. London and New York, 1966.

—— "Opacity in Actual Belief Structures," *The Journal of Philosophy* (forthcoming).

—— *Philosophy of Science*. New York, 1970.

Adams, E. M. "On Knowing That," *The Philosophical Quarterly 8* (1958), pp. 300–6.

Arbib, M. A. *The Metaphorical Brain*. New York, 1972.

Armstrong, David. "Does Knowledge Entail Belief?" *Proceedings of the Aristotelian Society 70* (1969), pp. 21–36.

Arner, Douglas. "On Knowing," *The Philosophical Review 68* (1959), pp. 84–92.

Aune, Bruce. *Knowledge, Mind, and Nature*. New York, 1967.

Austin, J. L. "Other Minds," in J. L. Austin, ed., *Philosophical Papers*. Oxford, 1961, pp. 44–84.

—— *Sense and Sensibilia*. Oxford and Fair Lawn, 1962.

Ayer, A. J. *The Problem of Knowledge*. London and Baltimore, 1956.

Barnes, W. H. F. "Knowing," *The Philosophical Review 72* (1963), pp. 3–16.

Brown, D. G. "Knowing How and Knowing That, What," in George Pitcher and Oscar P. Wood, eds., *Ryle.* New York, 1970, pp. 213–49.

Cargile, James. "A Note On 'Iterated Knowings,'" *Analysis 30* (1970), pp. 151–55.

Carnap, Rudolf. *Logical Foundations of Probability.* Chicago, 1950.

—— "Replies and Systematic Expositions," in P. A. Schilpp, ed., *The Philosophy of Rudolf Carnap.* La Salle, Illinois, 1963.

Castañeda, Hector-Neri. "On Knowing (or Believing) That One Knows (or Believes)," *Synthese 21* (1970), pp. 187–203.

—— "On The Logic of Self-Knowledge," *Nous 1* (1967), pp. 9–21.

Champawat, Narayan, and Saunders, Turk, John. "Mr. Clark's Definition of 'Knowledge,'" *Analysis 25* (1965), pp. 8–9.

Chisholm, Roderick. "Identity Through Possible Worlds: Some Questions," *Nous 1* (1967), pp. 1–8.

—— "On the Nature of Empirical Evidence," in Lawrence Foster, and I. W. Swanson, eds., *Experience and Theory.* Amherst, 1970, pp. 103–34.

—— *Perceiving: A Philosophical Study.* Ithaca, 1957.

—— "The Logic of Knowing," *The Journal of Philosophy 60* (1963), pp. 773–95.

Clark, Michael. "Knowing and Grounds: A Comment on Gettier's Paper," *Analysis 24* (1964), pp. 46–47.

Cohen, L. Jonathan. "More about Knowing and Feeling Sure," *Analysis 27* (1967), pp. 11–16.

Collins, Arthur W. "Unconscious Belief," *The Journal of Philosophy 66* (1969), pp. 667–80.

Cook, John W. "Wittgenstein on Privacy," *The Philosophical Review 74* (1965), pp. 281–314.

Danto, Arthur. *Analytical Philosophy of Knowledge*. Cambridge and New York, 1968.

Darmstadter, Howard. "Consistency of Belief," *The Journal of Philosophy 68* (1970), pp. 301–10.

Davidson, Donald. "Theories of Meaning and Learnable Languages," in Y. Bar-Hillel, ed., *Proceedings of the 1964 International Congress for Logic, Methodology, and Philosophy of Science*. Amsterdam, 1965, pp. 383–94.

Davidson, Donald, and Hintikka, Jaakko, eds., *Words and Objections: Essays on the Work of W. V. O. Quine*. Dordrecht and New York, 1969.

DeFinetti, Bruno. "Foresight: Its Logical Laws, Its Subjective Sources," in H. E. Kyburg, and Howard E. Smokler, eds., *Studies in Subjective Probability*. New York, 1964, pp. 93–158.

DeSousa, Ronald. "Knowledge, Consistent Belief, and Self-Consciousness," *The Journal of Philosophy 67* (1970), pp. 66–73.

Dretske, Fred I. "Epistemic Operators," *The Journal of Philosophy 67* (1970), pp. 1007–23.

Feldman, Shel, ed. *Cognitive Consistency*. New York, 1966.

Firth, R. "Chisholm and the Ethics of Belief," *The Philosophical Review 68* (1959), pp. 493–506.

Geach, P. T. "Assertion," *The Philosophical Review 74* (1965), pp. 449–65.

Gettier, Edmund L. "Is Justified True Belief Knowledge?" *Analysis 23* (1963), pp. 121–23.

Ginet, Carl. "What Must Be Added to Knowing to Obtain Knowing That One Knows?" *Synthese 21* (1970), pp. 163–86.

Goldman, Alvin I. "A Causal Theory of Knowing," *The Journal of Philosophy 64* (1967), pp. 357–72.

Harman, Gilbert. "Induction." In Marshall Swain, ed., *Induction, Acceptance and Rational Belief*. Dordrecht and New York, 1970, pp. 83–100.

——— "Knowledge, Inference, and Explanation," *American Philosophical Quarterly 5* (1968), pp. 164–73.

——— "Knowledge, Reasons, and Causes," *The Journal of Philosophy 67* (1970), pp. 841–55.

——— "Lehrer on Knowledge," *The Journal of Philosophy 63* (1966), pp. 241–46.

Harrison, Jonathan. "Does Knowing Imply Believing?" *The Philosophical Quarterly 15* (1963), pp. 322–32.

Hartland-Swann, J. " 'Being Aware of' and 'Knowing,' " *The Philosophical Quarterly 7* (1957), pp. 126–35.

——— "Logical Status of 'Knowing That,' " *Analysis 16* (1955), pp. 111–15.

Heidelberger, Herbert. "Knowledge, Certainty and Probability," *Inquiry 6* (1963), pp. 242–50.

——— "On Defining Epistemic Expressions," *The Journal of Philosophy 60* (1963), pp. 344–48.

Hilpinen, Risto. "Knowing That One Knows and the Classical Definition of Knowledge," *Synthese 21* (1970), pp. 109–32.

Hilpinen, Risto, and Hintikka, Jaakko. "Knowledge, Acceptance, and Inductive Logic," in J. Hintikka and P. Suppes, eds., *Aspects of Inductive Logic*. Amsterdam and New York, 1966, pp. 1–20.

Hintikka, Jaakko. "Individuals, Possible Worlds, and Epistemic Logic," *Nous 1* (1967), pp. 33–62.

—— " 'Knowing That One Knows' Reviewed," *Synthese 21* (1970), pp. 141–62.

—— *Knowledge and Belief*. Ithaca, 1962.

—— *Models for Modalities*. Dordrecht and New York, 1969.

—— "On Attributions of 'Self-Knowledge,' " *The Journal of Philosophy 67* (1970), pp. 73–87.

Hintikka, Jaakko, and Davidson, Donald, eds., *Words and Objections: Essays on the Work of W. V. O. Quine*. Dordrecht and New York, 1969.

Hintikka, Jaakko, and Hilpinen, Risto. "Knowledge, Acceptance, and Inductive Logic." In J. Hintikka, and P. Suppes, eds., *Aspects of Inductive Logic*. Amsterdam and New York, 1966, pp. 1–20.

Jeffrey, R. C. *The Logic of Decision*. New York, 1965.

Jeffrey, Isaac. "Probability and Evidence," in Marshall Swain, ed., *Induction, Acceptance, and Rational Belief*. Dordrecht and New York, 1970, pp. 157–85.

Kemeny, John G. "Carnap's Theory of Probability and Induction," in P. A. Schilpp, ed., *The Philosophy of Rudolf Carnap*. La Salle, Illinois, 1963.

Kiteley, Murray. "As Grammars of 'Believe,' " *The Journal of Philosophy 61* (1964), pp. 244–59.

Kyburg, Henry E. "Conjunctivitis," in Marshall Swain, ed., *Induction, Acceptance, and Rational Belief*. Dordrecht and New York, 1970, pp. 55–82.

Lehrer, Keith. "Belief and Knowledge," *The Philosophical Review 77* (1968), pp. 491–99.

—— "Believing That One Knows," *Synthese 21* (1970), pp. 133–40.

—— "Knowledge, Truth, and Evidence," *Analysis 25* (1965), pp. 168–75.

—— "The Fourth Condition of Knowledge: 'A Defense,'" *The Review of Metaphysics 24* (1970), pp. 122–28.

Lehrer, Keith, and Paxon, Thomas, Jr. "Knowledge: Undefeated Justified True Belief," *The Journal of Philosophy 66* (1969), pp. 225–37.

Lemmon, E. J. "If I Know, Do I Know That I Know?" in Avrum Stroll, ed., *Epistemology*. New York, 1967, pp. 54–82.

—— "Is There Only One Correct System of Modal Logic?" *Proceedings of the Aristotelian Society*, Suppl., Vol. 23 (1959), pp. 23–40.

Levi, Isaac. *Gambling With Truth*. New York, 1967.

—— "Justification, Explanation, and Induction," in Marshall Swain, ed., *Induction, Acceptance, and Rational Belief*. Dordrecht and New York, 1970, pp. 134–56.

Malcolm, Norman. "Knowledge and Belief," *Mind 61* (1952), pp. 178–89.

—— *Knowledge and Certainty: Essays and Lectures*. Englewood Cliffs, New Jersey, 1963.

Montague, Richard. "On the Nature of Certain Philosophical Entities," *The Mouist 53* (1969), pp. 159–94.

Odegard, D. "On Defining 'S Knows That p,'" *The Philosophical Quarterly 15* (1965), pp. 353–57.

Pailthorp, Charles. "A Reply to Lehrer," *The Review of Metaphysics 24* (1970), pp. 129–33.

—— "Knowledge As Justified True Belief," *The Review of Metaphysics 23* (1969), pp. 25–47.

Paxon, Thomas, Jr., and Lehrer, Keith. "Knowledge: Undefeated Justified True Belief," *The Journal of Philosophy 66* (1969), pp. 225–37.

Quine, W. V. O. *Word and Object.* New York, 1960.

Radford, Colin. "Does Unwitting Knowledge Entail Unconscious Belief?" *Analysis 30* (1970), pp. 103–7.

—— "Knowledge by Examples," *Analysis 27* (1966), pp. 1–11.

Ramsey, F. P. "Truth and Probability," reprinted in R. B. Braithwaite, ed., *The Foundations of Mathematics and Other Logical Essays by F. P. Ramsey.* New York, 1950.

Rokeach, Milton. *Beliefs, Attitudes, and Values.* San Francisco, 1968.

Rozeboom, William W. "Why I Know So Much More Than You Do," *American Philosophical Quarterly 4* (1967), pp. 281–90.

Ryle, Gilbert. *The Concept of Mind.* London and New York, 1949.

Rynin, David. "Knowledge, Sensation, and Certainty," in A. Stroll, ed., *Epistemology.* New York, 1967, pp. 10–31.

Saunders, Turk, John. "Does Knowledge Require Grounds?" *Philosophical Studies 17* (1966), pp. 7–13.

Saunders, Turk, John, and Champawat, Narayan. "Mr. Clark's Definition of 'Knowledge,'" *Analysis 25* (1965), pp. 8–9.

Savage, L. J. *Are Foundations of Statistics.* New York, 1954.

Scheffler, Israel. *Conditions of Knowledge*. Chicago, 1965.

Schick, Frederic. "Consistency," *The Philosophical Review 75* (1965), pp. 467–95.

—— "Consistency and Rationality," *The Journal of Philosophy 60* (1963), pp. 5–19.

—— "Three Logics of Belief," in Marshall Swain, ed., *Induction, Acceptance, and Rational Belief*. Dordrecht and New York, 1970, pp. 6–26.

Sellars, Wilfrid. "Some Problems about Belief," in J. W. Davis, D. J. Hockney, and W. K. Wilson, eds., *Philosophical Logic*. Dordrecht, 1969, pp. 46–65.

Skyrms, Brian. "The Explication of 'X Knows That p,'" *The Journal of Philosophy 64* (1967), pp. 373–89.

Sleigh, Robert C., Jr. "On a Proposed System of Epistemic Logic," *Nous 4* (1968), pp. 391–98.

—— "On Quantifying into Epistemic Contexts," *Nous 1* (1967), pp. 23–31.

Sosa, Ernest. "The Analysis of 'Knowledge That P,'" *Analysis 25* (1965), pp. 1–3.

—— "Propositional Knowledge," *Philosophical Studies 20* (1969), pp. 33–43.

—— "Quantifiers, Beliefs, and Sellars," in J. W. Davis, D. J. Hockney, and W. K. Wilson, eds., *Philosophical Logic*. Dordrecht and New York, 1969, pp. 66–73.

—— "Two Conceptions of Knowledge," *The Journal of Philosophy 67* (1970), pp. 59–66.

Stine, Gail. "Hintikka on Quantification and Belief," *Nous 3* (1969), pp. 399–408.

Swain, Marshall. "The Consistency of Rational Belief," in Marshall Swain, ed., *Induction, Acceptance, and Ra-*

tional Belief. Dordrecht and New York, 1970, pp. 27–54.

Swain, Marshall, ed., *Induction, Acceptance, and Rational Belief.* Dordrecht and New York, 1970.

Swartz, Robert. "Leibniz's Law and Belief," *The Journal of Philosophy 67* (1970), pp. 122–37.

Thalberg, Irving. "In Defense of Justified True Belief," *The Journal of Philosophy 66* (1969), pp. 794–803.

Unger, Peter. "A Defense of Skepticism," *The Philosophical Review 80* (1971), pp. 198–219.

—— "An Analysis of Factual Knowledge," *The Journal of Philosophy 65* (1968), pp. 157–70.

—— "Experience and Factual Knowledge," *The Journal of Philosophy 64* (1967), pp. 152–73.

Urmson, J. O. "Parenthetical Verbs," *Mind 61* (1952), pp. 480–96.

Vickers, John. "Some Features of Theories of Belief," *The Journal of Philosophy 68* (1966), pp. 197–201.

Wang, Hao. "A Question on Knowledge of Knowledge," *Analysis 14* (1953), pp. 142–46.

Woozley, A. D. "Knowing and Not Knowing," *Proceedings of the Aristotelian Society 53* (1952–53), pp. 151–72.

Index

(Note: Because of the large number of names involved, Bibliography entries are *not* included in the Index.)

20